Double Exposure

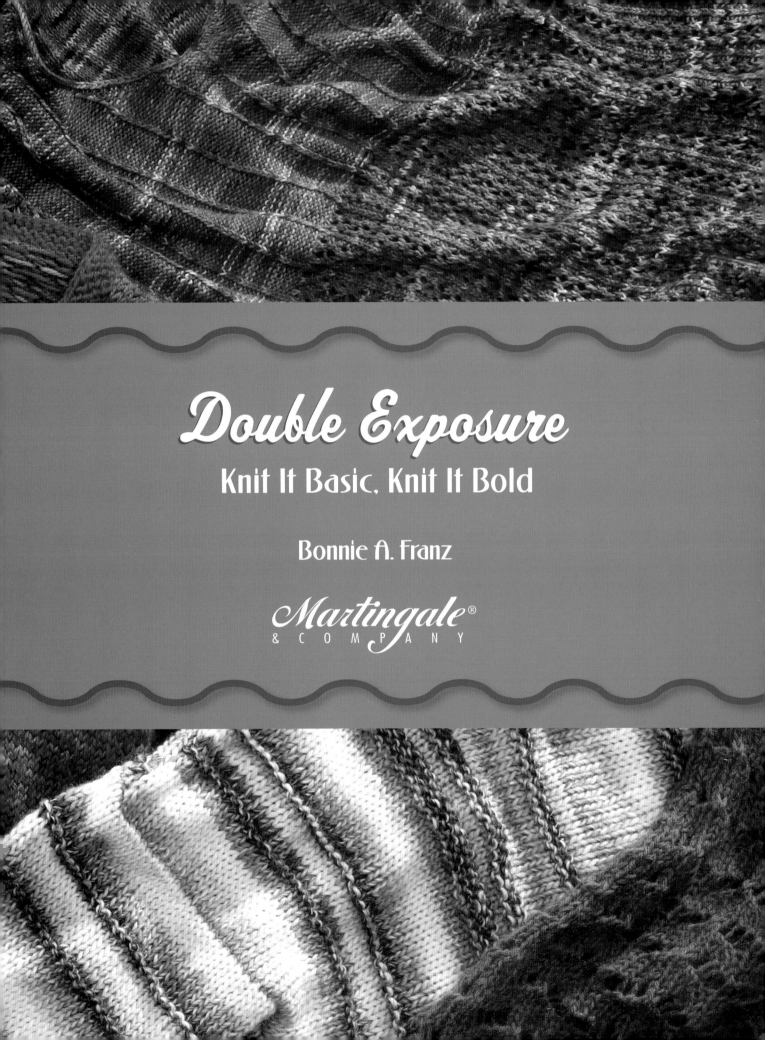

Double Exposure
Knit It Basic, Knit It Bold

Bonnie A. Franz

Martingale®
& COMPANY

Credits

President • Nancy J. Martin

CEO • Daniel J. Martin

COO • Tom Wierzbicki

Publisher • Jane Hamada

Editorial Director • Mary V. Green

Managing Editor • Tina Cook

Technical Editor • Ursula Reikes

Copy Editor • Sheila Chapman Ryan

Design Director • Stan Green

Illustrator • Robin Strobel

Cover and Text Designer • Shelly Garrison

Photographer • Brent Kane

Double Exposure: Knit It Basic, Knit It Bold
© 2006 by Bonnie A. Franz

Martingale & Company
20205 144th Avenue NE
Woodinville, WA 98072-8478 USA
www.martingale-pub.com

Printed in China
11 10 09 08 07 06   8 7 6 5 4 3 2 1

Library of Congress Cataloging-in-Publication Data

Library of Congress Control Number:
2006002358

ISBN-13: 978-1-56477-641-9
ISBN-10: 1-56477-641-7

Mission Statement

Dedicated to providing quality products
and service to inspire creativity.

Dedication

For Matthew

Acknowledgments

Completing this book would have been impossible without the help and support, in every way, of my parents and brother. Special thanks to Judy Seip and Donna Walker for their amazing knitting speed and skill. Thanks to all the owners and representatives of the yarn and button companies, and to the staff at Martingale & Company for help, support, and patience—especially Ursula Reikes and Sheila Ryan. Deep appreciation to Carole Wulster at Knitting Wizards and Janet Tombu at Knitware for their software, which made my job much easier.

Each sweater in this collection is named for a woman who has had an influence on my life or is in my family tree. Naming a sweater in their honor is a small thank-you or remembrance to Donna Yawman and Donna Ikefugi; Ruth Weckman; Marilyn Barge and Marilyn Laraia; Marie Dooley, May Flood, Mary Swift, Mary Trainor, and Mary Wheeler; Miranda Horan; Margaret Yawman, Margaret Kiernan, and Marguerite Rivas; Wendy Cavagnaro; Eleanor McGlynn; Jayne Robertson and Jayme Robertson; Alice Eastby; Virginia McGlynn; Pattie Brixen and Patsy James; Edna Franz; Ariel Horan; Maureen Franz; Rose Franz; Sandy Rhodes; Cecile McGlynn; Sue Wheeler, Susan Irvin and Sue LeMole; and Constance Franz.

Contents

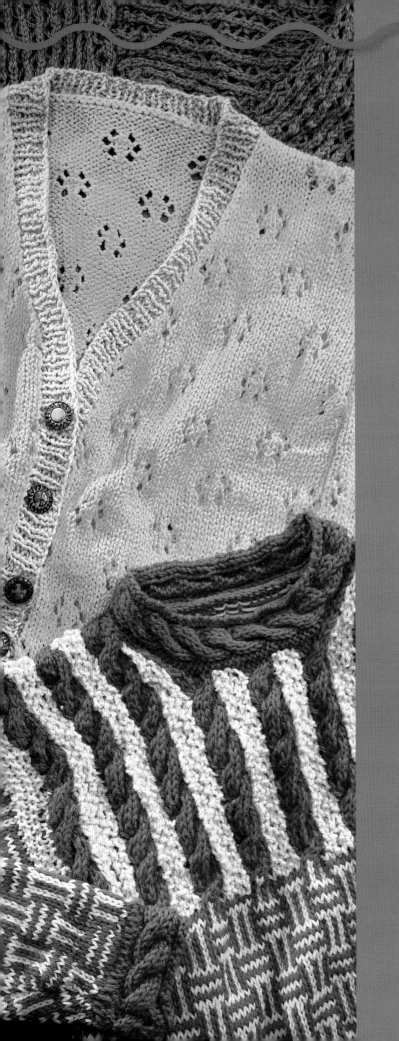

Introduction

It's often easy to get a clue about a person's personality from the colors she chooses to wear. Some people gravitate toward vibrant, dynamic colors while others tend toward the more subdued. I think we all have a need for both in our closets—the bold, bright pieces that serve as showstoppers and brighten our moods as we wear and knit them, as well as the comfortable, reliable neutrals that form the backbone of our wardrobes.

Of course, any sweater can be made in any color that inspires you, but I'm always reminded of the knitting legend of the woman who went to the yarn store looking for a pattern. The obliging shopkeeper showed her book after book of designs and encouraged her to browse the shop's collection of patterns in binders. Finally, the woman said she couldn't find anything she liked. The shopkeeper asked her to describe exactly what she was looking for, and the woman said, "Well, these patterns are all very nice, but what I'm really looking for is a pattern for a pink sweater."

I would hope that most knitters have enough imagination to "see" patterns in colors other than those used for the sample, but the

story does make a good point—very often our first response to a design is (consciously or not) influenced by the color of the sample.

I thought it would be useful for knitters to be able to see at a glance the drastic difference between a design worked in both a neutral palette and a vibrant one. Therefore, this book shows that by working a design you love in several different colors, you can produce a variety of looks.

I hope you'll see for yourself how easily the same piece can be worked one way to produce a wardrobe staple, and in another way to create a dramatic accent piece. In one person's case, gray might be a neutral, with purple as an accent. To another knitter, purple might be a mainstay with gray as an unusual jolt to the rest of the wardrobe.

Whether you gravitate toward the bold or the neutral, the vibrant or the subdued, I hope you find projects here to excite you. Before diving into the designs, read through the "Techniques" section (page 11) to see if there are any skills that are new to you. Then, choose your yarn and grab your needles. I encourage you to look at yarn choice as a way to double your knitting possibilities.

Techniques

Many of the designs in this book can be completed with only a basic knowledge of knitting. However, learning some variations of these skills can give your knits a more polished appearance. These techniques are meant to expand your knitting repertoire—they are not ironclad rules. You can certainly use your own preferred method for increasing, casting on, etc.

Backward-loop cast on. In Wendy Gansey (page 38), you will need to add a stitch at the end of some rows with the backward-loop cast on. Form a loop so that the yarn coming from the ball is in front of the yarn coming from the right-hand needle. Insert the needle into this loop and tighten gently.

Blocking. I'm pretty fearless about blocking. If an item is cotton, wool, linen, or bamboo, I usually steam press it with an ordinary iron. If an item is made in a yarn labeled "machine washable and dryable," I throw it in the washing machine and dryer. If an item is not made from one of the fibers listed above and is not machine washable or dryable, I hand wash it and lay it on a towel to dry. I strongly suggest testing your plan for blocking on your gauge swatch (page 14).

Casting on. Unless directed otherwise, use a long-tail cast on.

Decreasing. Unless directed otherwise, work all decreases one stitch away from the edge of the piece. This will give you a plain stitch on the edge to help in sewing pieces together or in picking up stitches for a trim.

I-Cord. Making I-cord can either be a soothing, Zenlike, mindless knitting experience or an endless, tiresome activity, depending on the knitter's point of view. To work, cast on three or four stitches on double-pointed needles. Do not turn. *Slide stitches to the other end of the needle and knit across, pulling the yarn across the back to form a tube. Repeat from * until desired length.

Alternative methods are to use a French or spool knitter (many of us had these as children; three or four nails at the top of a spool), or one of the knitting gadgets made for this purpose and available in craft stores. Machine knitters can whip out miles of I-cord in minutes, so if you truly hate making I-cord, check to see if you have a friend with a knitting machine. Whatever method you use, don't bind off the I-cord until you have stitched it to the piece so that you can ensure it is long enough.

Increasing. Unless directed otherwise, work all increases one stitch away from the edge of the piece. This will give you a plain stitch on the edge to help in sewing pieces together or in picking up stitches for a trim.

Knit into the front and back of same stitch (K1f&b). This creates two stitches out of one stitch. Knit into the next stitch but leave the stitch on the left needle. Then knit into the back of the same stitch and slip the old stitch off the left needle.

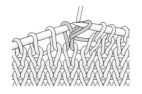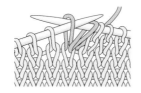

Make one increase (M1). This method creates a new stitch between two stitches. Insert the left-hand needle from front to back under the horizontal bar of yarn between two stitches. Knit into the back of this loop as though it were a stitch. Unless otherwise directed, use this increase method for all projects.

Picking up stitches. Always pick up stitches with the right side facing you unless otherwise instructed. The project directions will tell you how many stitches to pick up, but you may choose to make a piece longer, shorter, or wider than directed. In that case, if you're picking up stitches from a bound-off edge (for example, at the top or bottom of a piece), pick up one stitch for each stitch bound off. If you're picking up from a side edge, use your gauge as a guide. For example, if the gauge is three

stitches and five rows per inch, try to pick up three stitches for every five rows of knitting. Many knitters find it easiest to pick up stitches this way, and then increase or decrease in the first row to match the number of stitches given in a pattern. Practice on your swatch.

Picot row. A picot row gives a scalloped edge to your knitting. Work a few rows in stockinette stitch with a smaller needle, then change to larger needles and K1, *YO, K2tog, repeating from * to the last stitch, ending YO, K1. Work the rest of the piece, and while finishing, fold the edge at the YO/K2tog row, sewing the hem portion to the inside of the piece.

Provisional cast on. A provisional cast on leaves the stitches "live" so that they can be picked up and worked later in the directions. To work, use a length of waste yarn that is smooth and a different color from the yarn used for the project. Make a slipknot and hook the yarn with a crochet hook. *Holding the yarn and knitting needle in your left hand, wrap the yarn around the knitting needle. Use the crochet hook to pull the yarn through the loop of yarn on the hook. Repeat from * to form a chain with the required number of loops on the knitting needle. Cut the yarn and pull through the loop on the hook. When the piece is finished, undo this loop and "unzip" the chain, placing each stitch back on the needle.

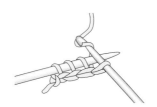

Sewn bind off. This should actually be called *mistake* sewn bind off since it's not the correct way to work a sewn bind off, but when I saw my mistake I liked the result so much that I left it. This bind off leaves a somewhat thick decorative edge. To work, cut the yarn approximately five times the width of the piece on the needles and thread it onto a tapestry needle. With the right side facing you and the knitting (still on the needle) in your left hand, take the yarn to the back of the piece and insert the tapestry needle from back to front through the fourth stitch from the end; pull the yarn to the front. Insert the tapestry needle as if to knit through the first stitch on the needle; pull the yarn to the back, pulling the yarn loosely at all times.* Remove the stitch from the needle. Bring the yarn to the front through the fifth stitch; bring the yarn to the back through the second stitch (which is now the first stitch). Repeat from *, moving one stitch to the left with each repetition. On the last three stitches, bring the yarn to the front through the last stitch.

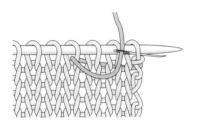

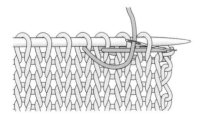

Short rows. Short rows are a method for working a part of a row so that the edge of the piece (often a shoulder) is slanted rather than straight when completed. Work as indicated in the directions.

Where the directions indicate "wrap st," if you're on a knitted row, slip the next stitch as if to purl with the yarn in back, move the yarn to the front, and return the slipped stitch to the left needle.

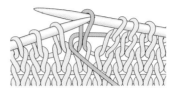

Slip stitch as if to purl. Move yarn to front of work and slip stitch back to left needle.

If you're on a purl row, slip the next stitch as if to purl with the yarn in front, move the yarn to the back, and return the slipped stitch to the left needle.

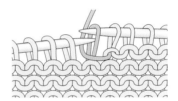

Slip stitch as if to purl. Move yarn to back of work and slip stitch back to left needle.

Either method will leave a little bar of yarn "hugging" the stitch. On the last row, when indicated in the directions, lift this bar and knit (or purl) it together with the stitch it was hugging.

Single crochet. You don't need to be a crocheter to work a basic crochet trim around a piece. To work, hold the knitting with the right side facing you and the yarn behind. Insert the crochet hook into a stitch in the knitting, hook the yarn, and pull it through the stitch toward you. Loop the yarn around the hook and pull through the loop on the hook. *Insert the hook into the next stitch, yarn over hook, and pull through the stitch. Loop the

13

yarn around the hook and pull through the loops on the hook. Repeat from * to the last stitch of knitting. Cut the yarn and pull through to end.

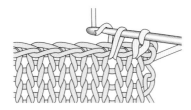

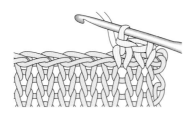

Steeks. Steeks are a method for creating openings in sweaters that are knitted completely in the round. Some people find knitting easier than purling, or they find that their gauges for knitting and purling are different and create an uneven fabric. Also, knitting in the round allows the knitter to see the pattern as it develops, catching potential color work errors. To make a steek, cast on the extra stitches designated in the directions. When the piece is completed, machine stitch two rows of zigzag stitching, one on top of the other, on both sides of the steek stitches and cut between them.

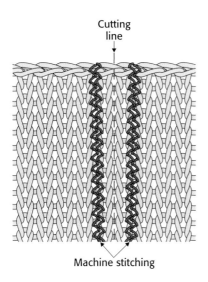

Cutting line

Machine stitching

Trim close to the stitching and tack the edges to the inside of the sweater if necessary. There are methods for steeking that don't involve a sewing machine, but I have had the best results using machine stitches.

If you'd like to try steeking but are nervous, try sewing and cutting a sweater from a thrift store, or practice on a large swatch. Your knitting is really much more stable than you think.

Gauge swatch. I cannot emphasize enough the importance of knitting a swatch before beginning a project. Work a pattern swatch that's at least 6" square. Use the exact yarn and needles you plan to use for the project and measure carefully to make sure you are getting the correct gauge. Change needles until your gauge matches the gauge in the directions. Then, I suggest you leave the swatch overnight and check it again. Use this swatch to test blocking methods, to practice picking up stitches or other techniques, to see if you like the color combination and texture of the swatch, and to see if you enjoy knitting the pattern before you commit yourself to a project. You can also take your swatch shopping with you to select buttons or other trims and add it to a notebook of projects you've done. Although it's tempting to dive right into a project and think you'll be right on gauge or at least close enough, resist the urge and work a swatch. I have a closet full of close-enough projects that weren't.

Three-needle bind off. Place the stitches of two pieces on two separate needles. Hold the pieces with right sides facing each other. *With a third needle, knit the first stitch from needle 1 and the first stitch from needle 2 together. Repeat from *, then pass the first stitch on the right-hand needle over the stitch you just made. Repeat across the row. When one stitch remains on the right-hand needle, cut a length of yarn and pull through the stitch to fasten off.

Tubular bind off. This is also called a grafted bind off in some reference books. It is only used with K1, P1 ribbing borders. After working a K1, P1 border, use two circular or double-pointed needles to place the knit stitches on one needle and the purl stitches on another. Cut a length of yarn approximately four times the width of the piece and thread it onto a tapestry needle.

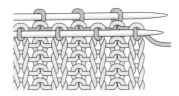

1. Draw the yarn through the first stitch on the front needle as if to purl; leave the stitch on the knitting needle. Draw the yarn through the first stitch on the back needle as if to knit; leave the stitch on the knitting needle.

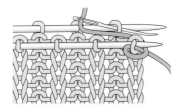

2. *Draw the yarn through the first stitch on the front needle as if to knit; then through the second stitch on the front needle as if to purl. Drop the first stitch off the front needle.

3. Draw the yarn through the first stitch on the back needle as if to purl; draw the yarn through the second stitch on the back needle as if to knit. Drop the first stitch off the back needle.

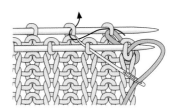

4. Repeat from * until one stitch remains on each needle. Draw the yarn through the stitch on the front needle as if to knit; drop it from the needle. Draw the yarn through the stitch on the back needle as if to purl; drop from the needle. Weave in the end.

Tubular cast on. Work the provisional cast on (page 12) for half the number of stitches needed plus one. When complete, join the project yarn. Knit one row, purl one row, and then knit one row. With the purl side facing you, *purl the first stitch; then insert the right-hand needle from top to bottom under the bar of the project yarn that's surrounded by waste yarn at the bottom of the piece.

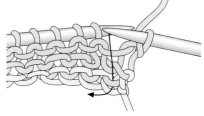

Lift this and place it on the left-hand needle by inserting the left needle from front to back into this bar. Knit this bar as a stitch. Repeat from *, ending with P1. On the next row, continue with K1, P1 ribbing as established.

Pullovers

Donna Sweater

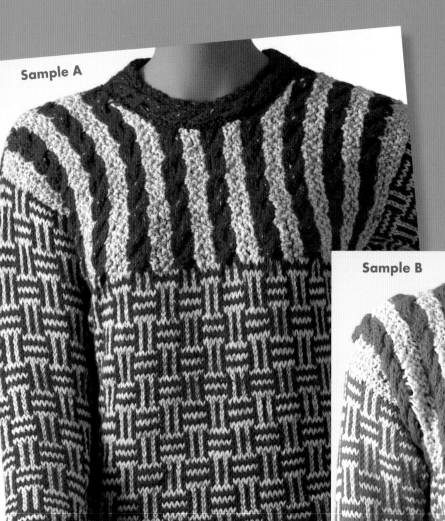

Sample A

Sample B

Some knitters love cable work. and others prefer color work. This sweater gives an opportunity to use both.

Yarn Notes: Although the combination of navy and ecru is considered neutral, you can see flecks of other colors spun into the yarns that liven up the look of the darker version. The eye is naturally drawn to shades of yellow, so the buttery yellow of the brighter version attracts attention.

Materials

Sample A

Galway Colornep from Plymouth Yarn Company (100% wool; 100 g; 210 yds) ❨4❩

MC 4 (4, 5, 6, 6, 7, 8) skeins • color 556

CC 4 (4, 5, 6, 6, 7, 8) skeins • color 501

Sample B

Galway from Plymouth Yarn Company (100% wool; 100 g; 210 yds) ❨4❩

MC 4 (4, 5, 6, 6, 7, 8) skeins • color 116

CC 4 (4, 5, 6, 6, 7, 8) skeins • color 104

Size 9 needles or size required to obtain gauge

Size 7 needles

Cable needle

Stitch markers

Gauge

18 sts and 18 rows = 4" in basket weave patt on larger needles

Basket Weave Pattern

Chart on page 22
(multiple of 10 + 5)

Row 1 (RS): *K5 CC, K1 MC, K1 CC, K1 MC, K1 CC, K1 MC, rep from * to last 5 sts, K5 CC.

Row 2: P5 MC, *P1 MC, P1 CC, P1 MC, P1 CC, P1 MC, P5 MC, rep from * to end.

Row 3: Rep row 1.

Row 4: Rep row 2.

Row 5: Rep row 1.

Row 6: P1 MC, P1 CC, P1 MC, P1 CC, P1 MC, *P5 CC, P1 MC, P1 CC, P1 MC, P1 CC, P1 MC, rep from * to end.

Row 7: *K1 MC, K1 CC, K1 MC, K1 CC, K1 MC, K5 MC, rep from * to last 5 sts, K1 MC, K1 CC, K1 MC, K1 CC, K1 MC.

Row 8: Rep row 6.

Row 9: Rep row 7.

Row 10: Rep row 6.

Rep rows 1–10 for patt.

Yoke Pattern

Chart on page 22
(multiple of 10 + 4)

C6F: Place next 3 sts on cn, hold in front, K3, K3 from cn.

Row 1 (RS): *With CC, K1, P1, K1, P1, with MC K6, rep from *, end with CC, K1, P1, K1, P1.

Row 2: With CC, P1, K1, P1, K1, *with MC P6, with CC, P1, K1, P1, K1, rep from * to end.

Row 3: *With CC, K1, P1, K1, P1, with MC C6F, rep from *, end with CC, K1, P1, K1, P1.

Row 4: Rep row 2.

Row 5: Rep row 1.

Row 6: Rep row 2.

Rep rows 1–6 for patt.

Cable Strip Pattern

Chart on page 22
(14 sts)

Use MC throughout

Row 1 (RS): K1, P3, K6, P3, K1.

Row 2: P1, K3, P6, K3, P1.

Row 3: K1, P3, C6F, P3, K1.

Row 4: Rep row 2.

Row 5: Rep row 1.

Row 6: Rep row 2.

Rep rows 1–6 for patt.

Back

With smaller needles and MC, CO 14 sts. Work 19 (21, 23¼, 25½, 27¾, 30, 32¼)" in cable strip patt. BO all sts. With larger needles, PU 85 (95, 105, 115, 125, 135, 145) sts along longer side. Purl 1 row with MC. Work in basket weave patt until basket weave portion measures 12 (12½, 13½, 14, 14, 14, 14)". Pm at each side to indicate under-arms. Work even in patt until armhole measures 9 (9, 10½, 11, 12, 13, 14)". BO all sts.

Front

Work as for back until basket weave portion measures 12 (12½, 13½, 14, 14, 14, 14)". Pm at each side to indicate underarms. Dec 1 st on next WS row. On next row, beg yoke patt and work until piece measures 20 (20½, 23, 23½, 24½, 25½, 26)" from beg. Work across 34 (38, 41, 46, 50, 55, 60) sts, attach another ball of yarn of each color, BO center 16 (18, 22, 22, 24, 24, 24) sts and finish row. Working both sides at same time, dec 1 st at neck edge EOR 5 (5, 5, 6, 6, 6, 7) times. Work even in patt until front is as long as back, BO rem 29 (33, 36, 40, 44, 49, 53) sts across each shoulder.

Sleeves (make 2)

With smaller needles and MC, CO 14 sts. Work 8 (8¼, 9½, 10½, 11½, 12½, 13)" in cable strip patt, BO all sts. With larger needles, PU 36 (38, 44, 48, 52, 56, 58) sts along longer side of strip. Purl 1 row with MC. Beg basket weave patt [last rep will have only 1 (3, 9, 3, 7, 1, 3) sts]. Working inc into patt, inc 1 st on each side of EOR 16 (0, 17, 18, 21, 24, 29) times, every 3 rows 0 (22, 0, 0, 0, 0, 0) times, then every 4 rows 7 (0, 8, 8, 7, 7, 5) times—82 (82, 94, 100, 108, 118, 126) sts. Work even until piece measures 16½ (16¾, 18, 18½, 19, 20, 20½)" from beg. BO all sts.

Finishing

Sew shoulder seams, sew sleeves to body, sew sleeve and side seams.

Neckband: Using MC and smaller needles, CO 14 sts and work cable strip patt until strip is long enough to reach around neckline, sew in place.

Weave in all ends and block as desired.

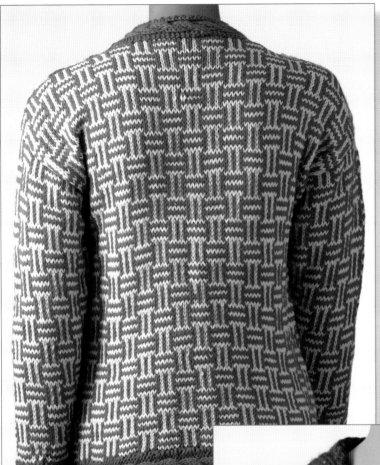

The back is worked entirely in
basket weave pattern.

A yoke pattern draws attention to the upper front.

Basket weave pattern

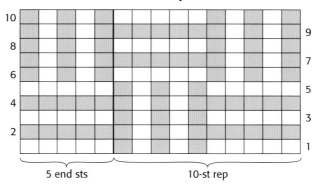

5 end sts   10-st rep

Yoke pattern

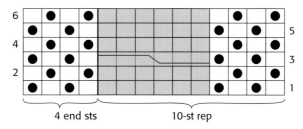

4 end sts   10-st rep

Cable strip pattern

Stitch key

☐ K on RS, P on WS

⬛ P on RS, K on WS

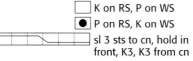 sl 3 sts to cn, hold in front, K3, K3 from cn

Color key

⬜ MC

☐ CC

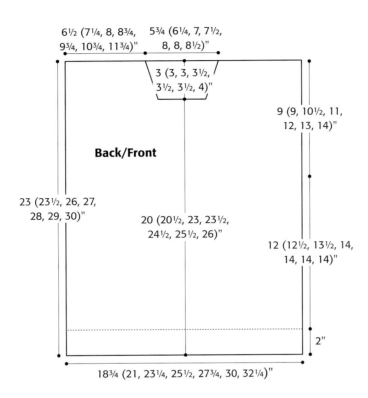

6½ (7¼, 8, 8¾, 9¾, 10¾, 11¾)"   5¾ (6¼, 7, 7½, 8, 8, 8½)"

3 (3, 3, 3½, 3½, 3½, 4)"

Back/Front

9 (9, 10½, 11, 12, 13, 14)"

23 (23½, 26, 27, 28, 29, 30)"

20 (20½, 23, 23½, 24½, 25½, 26)"

12 (12½, 13½, 14, 14, 14, 14)"

2"

18¾ (21, 23¼, 25½, 27¾, 30, 32¼)"

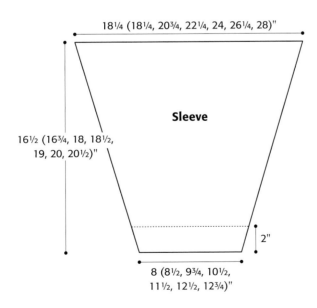

18¼ (18¼, 20¾, 22¼, 24, 26¼, 28)"

Sleeve

16½ (16¾, 18, 18½, 19, 20, 20½)"

2"

8 (8½, 9¾, 10½, 11½, 12½, 12¾)"

Marie Turtleneck

Very different yarn types produce very different draping results in this cabled turtleneck.

Sample A

Sample B

Skill Level: Experienced ◼◼◼◻

Size: Extra Small (Small, Medium/Large, 1X, 2X, 3X)

Finished Measurements:
Bust: 33½ (38½, 46½, 48½, 55, 62)"
Length: 24½ (26, 28, 29, 30, 32¼)"

Yarn Notes: The gray sweater is worked in a lightweight, shiny yarn. This soft, light yarn gives the fabric more drape, which means it is more flexible and will cling to your body more. The gold version is done in a heavy wool that has great body and texture. This heavier yarn will make a firmer fabric that will hold more of its own shape. The choice is yours.

Materials

Sample A

19 (19, 23, 25, 28, 33) skeins of Free Style Dalegarn from Dale of Norway (100% wool; 1¾ oz; 87 yds), color 2427 ⬡3⬡

Sample B

10 (10, 13, 14, 16, 17) skeins of Microspun from Lion Brand Yarn (100% microfiber acrylic; 2½ oz; 70 g; 168 yds; 154 m), color 149 Silver Grey ⬡3⬡

Size 4 needles or size required to obtain gauge

Size 3 needles

Size 3 circular needle (16") or double-pointed needles

Size 4 circular needle (16") or double-pointed needles

Stitch markers

Stitch holders

Cable needle

Gauge

One rep of central cable = 7" wide x 3⅓" high on larger needles

20 sts in zigzag patt = 3¼" wide x 3" high on larger needles

Zigzag Pattern

Chart on page 28
(multiple of 4 + 2)

RT: Sl next st to cn, hold in back, K1tbl, P1 from cn.

LT: Sl next st to cn, hold in front, P1, K1tbl from cn.

Row 1 (RS): P1, *P2, RT, rep from * to last st, P1.

Row 2: K1, *K1, P1tbl, K2, rep from * to last st, K1.

Row 3: P1, *P1, RT, P1, rep from * to last st, P1.

Row 4: K1, *K2, P1tbl, K1, rep from * to last st, K1.

Row 5: P1, *RT, P2, rep from * to last st, P1.

Row 6: K1, *K3, P1tbl, rep from * to last st, K1.

Row 7: P1, *LT, P2, rep from * to last st, P1.

Row 8: Rep row 4.

Row 9: P1, *P1, LT, P1, rep from * to last st, P1.

Row 10: Rep row 2.

Row 11: P1, *P2, LT, rep from * to last st, P1.

Row 12: K1, *P1tbl, K3, rep from * to last st, K1.

Rep rows 1–12 for patt.

Central Cable Pattern

Chart on page 28
(56 sts)

LC: Sl next 2 sts to cn, hold in front, P1, K2 from cn.

RC: Sl next st to cn, hold in back, K2, P1 from cn.

C4B: Sl next 2 sts to cn, hold in back, K2, K2 from cn.

C4F: Sl next 2 sts to cn, hold in front, K2, K2 from cn.

C6B: Sl next 3 sts to cn, hold in back, K3, K3 from cn.

C6F: Sl next 3 sts to cn, hold in front, K3, K3 from cn.

Row 1: P2, K12, P3, K2, P2, K2, P2, LC, RC, P2, K2, P2, K2, P3, K12, P2.

Row 2: K2, P12, K3, P2, K2, P2, K3, P4, K3, P2, K2, P2, K3, P12, K2.

Row 3: P2, C6B, C6B, P3, K2, P2, LC, P2, C4B, P2, RC, P2, K2, P3, C6F, C6F, P2.

Row 4: K2, P12, K3, P2, K3, P2, K2, P4, K2, P2, K3, P2, K3, P12, K2.

Row 5: P2, K12, P3, LC, P2, LC, RC, LC, RC, P2, RC, P3, K12, P2.

Row 6: K2, P12, K4, P2, K3, P4, K2, P4, K3, P2, K4, P12, K2.

Row 7: P2, K3, C6F, K3, P4, LC, P2, C4F, P2, C4F, P2, RC, P4, K3, C6B, K3, P2.

Row 8: K2, P12, K5, P2, K2, P4, K2, P4, K2, P2, K5, P12, K2.

Row 9: P2, K12, P5, LC, RC, LC, RC, LC, RC, P5, K12, P2.

Row 10: K2, P12, K6, P4, K2, P4, K2, P4, K6, P12, K2.

Row 11: P2, C6B, C6B, P6, C4B, P2, C4B, P2, C4B, P6, C6F, C6F, P2.

Row 12: K2, P12, K6, P4, K2, P4, K2, P4, K6, P12, K2.

Row 13: P2, K12, P5, RC, LC, RC, LC, RC, LC, P5, K12, P2.

Row 14: K2, P12, K5, P2, K2, P4, K2, P4, K2, P2, K5, P12, K2.

Row 15: P2, K3, C6F, K3, P4, RC, P2, C4F, P2, C4F, P2, LC, P4, K3, C6B, K3, P2.

Row 16: K2, P12, K4, P2, K3, P4, K2, P4, K3, P2, K4, P12, K2.

Row 17: P2, K12, P3, RC, P2, RC, LC, RC, LC, P2, LC, P3, K12, P2.

Row 18: K2, P12, K3, P2, K3, P2, K2, P4, K2, P2, K3, P2, K3, P12, K2.

Row 19: P2, C6B, C6B, P3, K2, P2, RC, P2, C4B, P2, LC, P2, K2, P3, C6F, C6F, P2.

Row 20: K2, P12, K3, P2, K2, P2, K3, P4, K3, P2, K2, P2, K3, P12, K2.

Row 21: P2, K12, P3, K2, P2, K2, P2, RC, LC, P2, K2, P2, K2, P3, K12, P2.

Row 22: K2, P12, K3, P2, K2, P2, K2, P2, K2, P2, K2, P2, K3, P12, K2.

Row 23: P2, K3, C6F, K3, P3, K2, P2, K2, P2, K2, P2, K2, P2, K3, P3, K3, C6F, K3, P2.

Row 24: K2, P12, K3, P2, K2, P2, K2, P2, K2, P2, K2, P2, K3, P12, K2.

Rep rows 1–24 for patt.

Sleeve Cable Pattern

Chart on page 28
(14 sts)

Row 1 (RS): P2, K12, P2.

Row 2 and all WS rows: K2, P12, K2.

Row 3: P2, C6B, C6B, P2.

Row 5: Rep row 1.

Row 7: P2, K3, C6F, K3, P2.

Row 8: K2, P12, K2.

Rep rows 1–8 for patt.

Back

With smaller needles, CO 104 (116, 140, 148, 160, 180) sts. Work in K2, P2 ribbing for 3" ending with WS row. On next RS row, change to larger needles and inc 12 (16, 16, 16, 20, 24) sts evenly spaced across row—116 (132, 156, 164, 180, 204) sts. Purl 1 row, pm on either side of center 56 sts. Working outer sections in zigzag patt and center section in central cable patt, work in patt until piece measures 14½ (15½, 16, 16½, 16½, 17)" from beg, pm at each end to indicate underarm. Work in patt until piece measures 23½ (25, 27, 28, 29, 31¼)" from beg. BO 38 (46, 54, 58, 63, 73) sts across each shoulder and place center 40 (40, 48, 48, 54, 58) sts on holder.

Front

Work as for back until body measures 20½ (22, 24, 24½, 25½, 26¾)" from beg.

Shape neck: Work in patt across 48 (55, 63, 69, 74, 86) sts, place center 20 (22, 30, 26, 32, 32) sts on holder. Join a second ball of yarn and finish row. Working both sides at same time, dec 1 st at each neck edge EOR 10 (9, 9, 11, 11, 13) times. Work even in patt until front piece matches back length. BO 38 (46, 54, 58, 63, 73) sts on each shoulder.

Sleeves (Make 2)

With smaller needles, CO 44 (48, 56, 60, 68, 72) sts. Work in K2, P2 ribbing for 2½" ending with WS row. On next RS row change to larger needles and inc 6 (8, 6, 8, 6, 10) sts evenly spaced across row—50 (56, 62, 68, 74, 82) sts. Purl 1 row, pm on either side of center 16 sts. Work outer sections in zigzag patt and center section in sleeve cable patt, working inc into patt, inc 1 st at each end of EOR 30 (27, 37, 35, 38, 49) times, then every 4 rows 7 (10, 6, 8, 8, 4) times—124 (130, 148, 154, 166, 188) sts. When sleeve measures 16½ (17½, 18, 18½, 19½, 20½)" from beg, BO outer sections and cont sleeve cable patt on center 16 sts until this section measures 6¼ (7½, 8½, 9¼, 10, 11¾)" from bound-off sections. Place these sts on a holder.

Finishing

Sew shoulders tog with cable from sleeve between front and back shoulders; leave cable sts on holder as you do this. With smaller circular needle, PU 16 sts from left sleeve top holder, 13 (13, 15, 15, 19, 17) sts from left neck edge, 20 (22, 26, 32, 28, 32) sts from front neck holder, 13 (13, 15, 15, 19, 17) sts from right front neck edge, 16 sts from right sleeve top holder, and 34 (40, 48, 54, 50, 58) sts from back neck holder—112 (120, 136, 148, 148, 156) sts. Join into rnd, being careful not to twist, pm to indicate start of rnd. Work in K2, P2 ribbing for 3", BO for mock turtleneck version or change to larger needles and cont in ribbing for another 3" for full turtleneck, BO all sts loosely in ribbing. Sew sleeves to body, sew sleeve and side seams. Weave in all ends and block as desired.

Sleeve cable at top of sleeve and shoulder.

Stitch key

☐	K or RS, P on WS
●	P on RS, K on WS
B	K tbl on RS, P tbl on WS
B ●	Left twist (LT): sl 1 st to cn, hold in front, P1, K1tbl from cn
● B	Right twist (RT): sl 1 st to cn, hold in back, K1tbl, P1 from cn
	Left cross (LC): sl 2 sts to cn, hold in front, P1 K2 from cn
	Right cross (RC): sl 2 sts to cn, hold in back, K2, P1 from cn
	C4B: sl 2 sts to cn, hold in back, K2, K2 from cn
	C4F: sl 2 sts to cn, hold in front, K2, K2 from cn
	C6B: sl 3 sts to cn, hold in back, K3, K3 from cn
	C6F: sl 3 sts to cn, hold in front, K3, K3 from cn

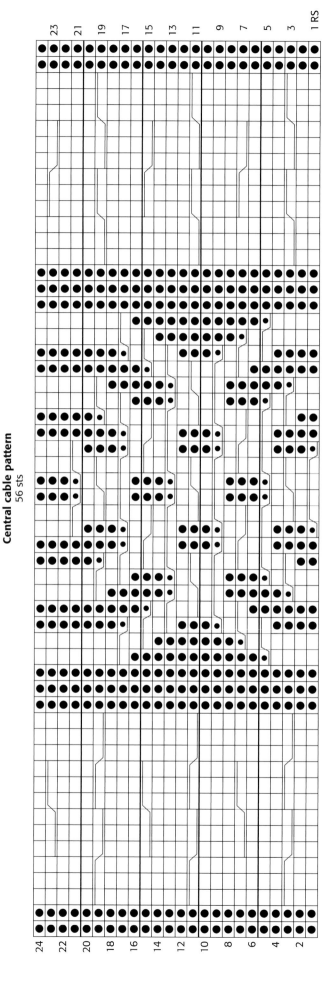

Central cable pattern
56 sts

Sleeve cable pattern
14 sts

Zigzag pattern

End st   4 st rep   Beg st

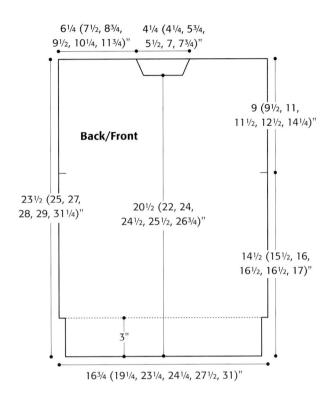

6¼ (7½, 8¾, 9½, 10¼, 11¾)"   4¼ (4¼, 5¾, 5½, 7, 7¾)"

Back/Front

9 (9½, 11, 11½, 12½, 14¼)"

23½ (25, 27, 28, 29, 31¼)"

20½ (22, 24, 24½, 25½, 26¾)"

14½ (15½, 16, 16½, 16½, 17)"

3"

16¾ (19¼, 23¼, 24¼, 27½, 31)"

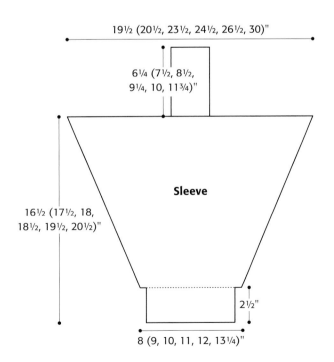

19½ (20½, 23½, 24½, 26½, 30)"

6¼ (7½, 8½, 9¼, 10, 11¾)"

Sleeve

16½ (17½, 18, 18½, 19½, 20½)"

2½"

8 (9, 10, 11, 12, 13¼)"

Miranda Top

The solid top of this sweater provides coverage. while the lace pattern below keeps you cool and feminine.

Sample A

Sample B

Size: Extra Small (Small, Medium, Large, 1X, 2X, 3X)

Finished Measurements:
Bust: 37½ (42, 46, 50½, 54½, 57, 63½)"
Length: 22¾ (24¼, 24¾, 26¼, 27¼, 29¾, 30¾)"

Yarn Notes: While working with bamboo yarn may sound exotic, knitting with it is actually quite similar to working with soft cotton, silk, or prewashed linen. Bamboo is absorbent so it takes color extremely well, and breathes like cotton or linen, making it very comfortable to wear for summer pieces.

Materials

7 (9, 10, 11, 13, 15, 17) skeins of Bamboo from Alchemy Yarns of Transformation (100% bamboo; 50 g; 138 yds) (2)

Sample A color 40M Madre Deus

Sample B color 26A Empty Sky

Size 4 needles or size required to obtain gauge

Size 3 circular needle (16")

Gauge

26 sts and 36 rows = 4" in openwork patt on larger needles

Openwork Pattern

(multiple of 7 + 3)

Row 1 (RS): *P1, K1tbl, P1, K2tog, YO, K2tog, YO, rep from * to last 3 sts, P1, K1tbl, P1.

Row 2: K1, P1, K1, *P4, K1, P1, K1, rep from * to end.

Row 3: *P1, K1tbl, P1, YO, ssk, YO, ssk, rep from * to last 3 sts, P1, K1tbl, P1.

Row 4: Rep row 2.

Rep rows 1–4 for patt.

Solid Pattern

(multiple of 7 + 3)

Row 1 (RS): *P1, K1tbl, P5, rep from * to last 3 sts, P1, K1tbl, P1.

Row 2: K1, P1, K1, *K5, P1, K1, rep from * to end.

Rep rows 1 and 2 for patt.

Back

With larger needles, CO 122 (136, 150, 164, 178, 185, 206) sts. Work in openwork patt until piece measures 11" from beg. Change to solid patt and work until piece measures 14 (15, 15, 16, 16, 16, 16)" from beg.

Shape armhole: BO 8 (11, 13, 15, 17, 18, 21) sts at beg of next 2 rows. Dec 1 st at each side EOR 7 (11, 13, 15, 17, 17, 20) times—92 (92, 98, 104, 110, 115, 124) sts. Work even in patt until piece measures 22 (23½, 24, 25½, 26½, 29, 30)" from beg.

Shape shoulders and back neck (see "Short Rows" on page 13) as follows:

Rows 1 and 2: Work to last 8 (9, 9, 10, 10, 11, 12) sts, wrap next st on left needle and turn.

Row 3: Work across 16 (18, 19, 19, 21, 22, 24) sts, join second ball of yarn and BO 36 (38, 42, 46, 48, 49, 52) sts for back neck, work to last 16 (18, 18, 19, 20, 22, 24) sts, wrap next st on left needle and turn.

Row 4: Work to last 16 (18, 18, 19, 20, 22, 24) sts, wrap next st on left needle and turn.

Row 5: Dec 1 st at neck edge, work across shoulder sts, PU wraps, turn.

Row 6: Work across row, PU rem wraps.

Place sts on holder. Rep on second shoulder.

Front

Work as for back, including beg armhole shaping, and AT SAME TIME when piece measures 14¾ (15¾, 15¾, 16¾, 16¾, 16¾, 16¾)" from beg, work across 53 (57, 62, 67, 72, 74, 82) sts, join second ball of yarn and BO 0 (0, 0, 0, 0, 1, 0) sts, finish row. Working both sides at once, dec 1 st at each neck edge EOR 7 (20, 22, 13, 11, 0, 0) times, every 4 rows 12 (0, 0, 11, 14, 24, 26) times, then every 6 rows 0 (0, 0, 0, 0, 1, 1) times. Cont even in solid patt until piece measures 22 (23½, 24, 25½, 26½, 29, 30)" from beg.

Shape shoulders: Work shoulders as for back.

Sleeves (Optional—Make 2)

With larger needles, CO 74 (78, 78, 104, 118, 118, 130) sts. Beg openwork patt and working incs into patt, inc 1 st at each side every row 0 (0, 12, 0, 0, 0, 0) times, EOR 12 (14, 8, 0, 0, 25, 25) times, every 4 rows 3 (2, 0, 7, 4, 1, 1) times, then every 6 rows 0 (0, 0, 3, 5, 0, 0) times—104 (110, 118, 124, 136, 170, 182) sts. Cont even in patt until piece measures 4 (4, 4, 5, 5, 6, 6)" from beg.

Shape cap: BO 8 (11, 13, 15, 17, 18, 21) sts at beg of next 2 rows. Dec 1 st at each side EOR 7 (11, 13, 15, 17, 17, 20) times, every row 17 (10, 9, 4, 2, 7, 5) times, then EOR 3 (6, 6, 8, 10, 15, 16) times. BO 4 (4, 4, 5, 5, 7, 7) sts at beg of next 4 rows. BO rem 18 (18, 20, 20, 24, 28, 30) sts.

Finishing

Use 3-needle BO (page 14) to join shoulders. Sew sleeves (if applicable) to body, sew side and sleeve seams. With smaller needles, PU 158 (158, 170, 180, 196, 236, 250) sts around neck edge, BO all sts. If sleeves are not used, PU 110 (110, 116, 124, 136, 168, 182) sts around each armhole edge, BO all sts. Weave in all ends and block as desired.

With sleeves or without, this sweater is sure to be a warm-weather favorite.

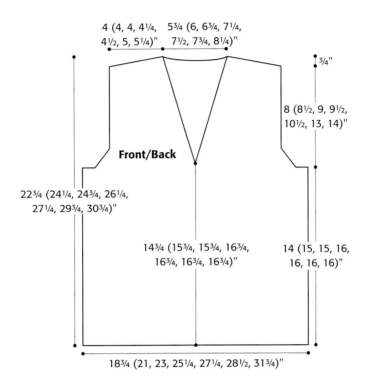

4 (4, 4, 4¼, 4½, 5, 5¼)"   5¾ (6, 6¾, 7¼, 7½, 7¾, 8¼)"

¾"

8 (8½, 9, 9½, 10½, 13, 14)"

Front/Back

22¾ (24¼, 24¾, 26¼, 27¼, 29¾, 30¾)"

14¾ (15¾, 15¾, 16¾, 16¾, 16¾, 16¾)"   14 (15, 15, 16, 16, 16, 16)"

18¾ (21, 23, 25¼, 27¼, 28½, 31¾)"

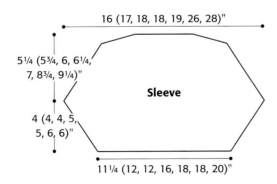

16 (17, 18, 18, 19, 26, 28)"

5¼ (5¾, 6, 6¼, 7, 8¾, 9¼)"

Sleeve

4 (4, 4, 5, 5, 6, 6)"

11¼ (12, 12, 16, 18, 18, 20)"

Margaret Rolled-Edge Pullover

The yarn does the work in this cozy pullover. It's knit side to side, which creates flattering vertical stripes.

Sample A

Sample B

Skill Level: Beginner ◖■■▶

Size: Extra Small (Small, Medium, Large, 1X, 2X, 3X)

Finished Measurements:
Bust: 38 (43, 47, 51, 55, 59, 63)"
Length: 19 (22, 23½, 24½, 25½, 26½, 27½)"
excluding bottom rolled edge

Yarn Notes: Yarn selection is crucial to this design because the yarn will be doing most of the work. Choose a variegated yarn that has long stretches of each color. The yarn I used is bulky weight, but very light. If you substitute yarns, be sure the weight of the finished sweater won't change your gauge. To check, hang some weights on your swatch for a few days and recheck.

Materials

Di.Vé Teseo from Cascade Yarns (55% wool, 45% microfiber; 1¾ oz; 98 yds) ⑤

Sample A (Refer to "Yarn Notes" above.)

9 (12, 14, 15, 17, 18, 20) balls • color 39361

Sample B (Refer to "Yarn Notes" above.)

9 (12, 14, 15, 17, 18, 20) balls • color 24899

Size 9 needles or size required to obtain gauge

Size 7 needles

Gauge

14¾ sts and 22 rows = 4" in patt st on larger needles

Stripe Pattern

To work the stripe patt, choose one of the colors within the variegation (in each of the samples, I chose the darkest color). When you reach that color as you're knitting, work all the stitches of that color in rev St st. While it may be difficult to tell exactly where one color ends and the next one begins, don't worry too much about starting at the perfect spot. Your sweater will look different depending on which color you choose for the rev St st section, so try swatching each possibility and see which you like best.

Back

With larger needles, CO 70 (81, 87, 91, 94, 98, 102) sts, work in stripe patt until piece measures 19 (21½, 23½, 25½, 27½, 29½, 31½)" from beg. BO all sts.

Front

Work as for back until piece measures 6¼ (7½, 8¼, 9, 9¾, 10¾, 11½)" ending with WS row.

Shape neck

Row 1: BO 1 st, finish row.

Row 2: Work to last 3 sts, P2tog, P1.

Row 3: BO 2 sts, finish row.

Row 4: Rep row 2.

For Large, 1X, and 2X, rep row 1 once; for 3X rep rows 1 and 2 once—65 (76, 82, 85, 88, 92, 95) sts.

Work even in patt for 26 (26, 28, 31, 33, 33, 32) rows, ending on WS row.

Row 1: K1, M1, finish row.

Row 2: Work to last 2 sts, M1, P1.

Row 3: CO 2 sts, finish row.

A rolled neck edge adds to the casual feel of this design.

Row 4: Rep row 2.

For Large, 1X, and 2X, rep row 1 once; for 3X, rep rows 1 and 2 once—70 (81, 87, 91, 94, 98, 102) sts.

Work even in patt until piece measures 19 (21½, 23½, 25½, 27½, 29½, 31½)" from beg. BO all sts.

Sleeves (Make 2)

With smaller needles, CO 30 (34, 36, 40, 42, 46, 48) sts. Work in St st for 2½" (edge will roll). Change to larger needles, beg stripe patt, and inc 1 st at each side EOR 0 (0, 2, 1, 3, 5, 9) times, every 4 rows 2 (16, 19, 20, 20, 20, 19) times, then every 6 rows 13 (2, 0, 0, 0, 0, 0) times—64 (74, 78, 82, 88, 96, 104) sts. Work even in patt until piece measures 16¾ (17½, 18, 18½, 19, 20, 20½)" from bottom of rolled edge. BO all sts.

Finishing

Sew one shoulder seam. With smaller needles PU 84 (84, 90, 96, 104, 104, 110) sts around neck edge. Work 3" in St st. BO all sts loosely. With smaller needles, PU 93 (105, 115, 125, 135, 145, 155) sts across bottom edge of front. Work 3" in St st and BO sts. Rep across bottom edge of back. Sew shoulder seam and neck edge, sew sleeves to body, sew sleeve and side seams. Weave in all ends and block as desired. If you want, tack rolled edge from inside of sweater to keep the roll in place.

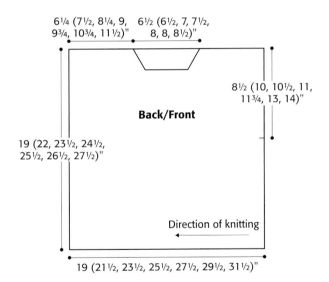

6¼ (7½, 8¼, 9, 9¾, 10¾, 11½)" 6½ (6½, 7, 7½, 8, 8, 8½)"

8½ (10, 10½, 11, 11¾, 13, 14)"

Back/Front

19 (22, 23½, 24½, 25½, 26½, 27½)"

Direction of knitting

19 (21½, 23½, 25½, 27½, 29½, 31½)"

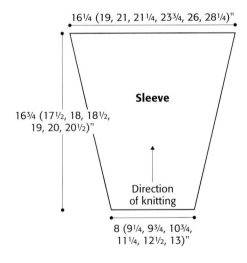

16¼ (19, 21, 21¼, 23¾, 26, 28¼)"

Sleeve

16¾ (17½, 18, 18½, 19, 20, 20½)"

Direction of knitting

8 (9¼, 9¾, 10¾, 11¼, 12½, 13)"

Wendy Gansey

Sample A

Sample B

Lace and texture combine to create a feminine version of the traditional gansey form.

Skill Level: Intermediate ⬛⬛⬛▭

Size: Extra Small/Small (Medium, Large, 1X, 2X, 3X)

Finished Measurements:
Bust: 39 (43, 47, 51, 55, 59)"
Length: 23¾ (24¾, 25¾, 26¼, 27¾, 30¼)"

Yarn Notes: A substantial tweed wool gives this design a knobby texture and body for a more rugged effect. The mohair version creates a soft, cozy feel and delicate effect. The tweed version will maintain its shape, while the mohair version will cling to your shape. Choose the one you prefer, or make one of each.

Materials

Sample A

5 (6, 7, 7, 8, 9) skeins of Yorkshire Tweed Aran from Rowan Yarns (100% wool; 100 g; 175 yds), color 414 Darkside 🔵4

Sample B

6 (7, 8, 8, 9, 11) skeins of Kid Classic from Rowan Yarns (70% lambs' wool, 26% kid mohair, 4% nylon; 50 g; 151 yds), color 844 Frilly 🔵4

Size 9 needles or size required to obtain gauge

Size 9 circular needle (16" long) or double-pointed needles

Size 7 needles

Stitch holders

Gauge

13⅓ sts and 20 rows = 4" in lace patt st on larger needles

Lace Pattern

(multiple of 8)

> When the final repeat in a row ends with a YO, do a backward-loop CO (page 11) to CO 1 st instead of working the YO.

Row 1 (RS): *K1, YO, ssk, K3, K2tog, YO, rep from *.

Row 2: *P1, YO, ssp, P1, P2tog, YO, P2, rep from *.

Row 3: *K3, YO, sl 1, K2tog, psso, YO, K2, rep from *.

Row 4: Purl.

Row 5: Knit.

Row 6: Purl.

Rep rows 1–6 for patt.

Yoke Pattern

(multiple of 4)

Rows 1 and 2: *K2, P2, rep from *.

Rows 3 and 4: *P2, K2, rep from *.

Rep rows 1–4 for patt.

Back

With smaller needles CO 72 (80, 88, 88, 96, 104) sts. Work 6 rows in garter st. Change to larger needles and beg lace patt, dec 1 st at each side every 23 (18, 15, 38, 39, 26) rows 2 (2, 4, 1, 2, 3) times, every 24 (19, 16, 0, 0, 0) rows 1 (2, 1, 0, 0, 0) time—66 (72, 78, 86, 92, 98) sts. Work even in patt until piece measures 14½ (15, 15½, 15½, 16, 16)" from beg ending with RS row.

Shape armholes: BO 5 (6, 7, 7, 8, 10) sts at beg of next 2 rows. Knit 1 row. Beg yoke patt and dec 1 st at each side EOR 5 (6, 7, 9, 10, 10) times—46 (48, 50, 54, 56, 58) sts. Work even in patt until piece measures 22½ (23½, 24½, 25, 26½, 29)" from beg.

Shape shoulders: BO 4 sts at beg of next 6 (4, 4, 2, 0, 0) rows. BO 5 sts at beg of next 0 (2, 2, 4, 6, 6) rows. Place rem 22 (22, 24, 26, 26, 28) sts on holder.

Front

Work as for back until piece measures 21¾ (22¾, 23¾, 23¾, 25¼, 26¾)". Work across 15 (17, 17, 18, 19, 22) sts, place center 16 (14, 16, 18, 18, 14) sts on holder, join second ball of yarn and finish row. Working both sides at same time, dec 1 st at each neck edge EOR 3 (4, 4, 4, 4, 7) times. Work even in patt until piece measures 22½ (23½, 24½, 25, 26½, 29)" from beg. Work shoulder shaping as for back.

Sleeves (Make 2)

With smaller needles, CO 48 (48, 56, 56, 64, 72) sts. Work 6 rows in garter st. Change to larger needles and beg lace patt. Working incs into patt, inc 1 st on each side of every 16 rows 3 (3, 2, 4, 3, 0) times, every 18 rows 0 (2, 0, 0, 0, 0) times, then every 9 rows 0 (0, 0, 0, 0, 8) times—54 (58, 60, 64, 70, 88) sts. Work even until piece measures 16¾ (17½, 17½, 16, 16½, 17½)" from beg.

Shape cap: BO 5 (6, 7, 8, 9, 10) sts at beg of next 2 rows. Dec 1 st at each side EOR 5 (6, 7, 8, 8, 10) times, every row 6 (7, 5, 5, 4, 6) times, then EOR 2 (1, 2, 2, 4, 5) times. BO 2 (2, 2, 2, 2, 3) sts at beg of next 4 rows. BO rem 10 (10, 10, 10, 12, 14) sts.

Finishing

Sew one shoulder seam.

Neckband: With smaller needles, PU 54 (54, 58, 68, 68, 80) sts around neck edge, including sts on holders. Work 4 rows in garter st, BO all sts loosely.

Sew rem shoulder and neckband. Sew sleeves to body, sew sleeve and side seams. Weave in all ends and block as desired.

The gentle shaping of the body and the loose sleeves add to the feminine allure.

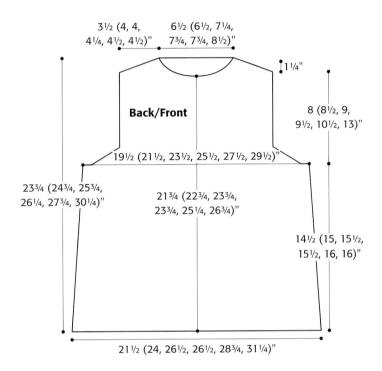

3½ (4, 4, 4¼, 4½, 4½)"

6½ (6½, 7¼, 7¾, 7¾, 8½)"

1¼"

Back/Front

8 (8½, 9, 9½, 10½, 13)"

19½ (21½, 23½, 25½, 27½, 29½)"

23¾ (24¾, 25¾, 26¼, 27¾, 30¼)"

21¾ (22¾, 23¾, 23¾, 25¼, 26¾)"

14½ (15, 15½, 15½, 16, 16)"

21½ (24, 26½, 26½, 28¾, 31¼)"

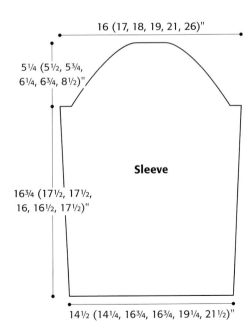

16 (17, 18, 19, 21, 26)"

5¼ (5½, 5¾, 6¼, 6¾, 8½)"

Sleeve

16¾ (17½, 17½, 16, 16½, 17½)"

14½ (14¼, 16¾, 16¾, 19¼, 21½)"

Ariel Pullover

Sample A

This is a cozy sweater
for cold weather.

Sample B

Yarn Notes: Both versions of this sweater are knit in a blend of silk, alpaca, and merino wool. Silk contributes shine, alpaca adds softness, and merino wool provides warmth. All three fibers take dye exceptionally well. The combination provides warmth without weight. Although the multicolored version looks more complicated, you're still only using two colors in any row.

Materials

Andean Silk from Knit Picks (55% superfine alpaca, 23% silk, 22% merino wool; 50 g; 96 yds) ❨4❩

Sample A

MC 8 (10, 12, 13, 14, 16) skeins • color Cinnamon

CC 8 (10, 12, 13, 14, 16) skeins • color Cream

Sample B

MC 4 (5, 6, 7, 8, 8) skeins • color Pitch

CC1 3 (4, 4, 5, 5, 6) skeins • color Yarrow

CC2 3 (4, 4, 5, 5, 6) skeins • color Chocolate

CC3 3 (4, 4, 5, 5, 6) skeins • color Orange

CC4 3 (4, 4, 5, 5, 6) skeins • color Mustard

Size 7 needles or size required to obtain gauge

Size 5 straight needles and size 5 circular needle (16") or double-pointed needles

Gauge

18 sts and 18 rows = 4" in patt st on larger needles

Corrugated Ribbing Pattern

(multiple of 4)

Row 1 (RS): *K2 with MC, P2 with CC, rep from *.

Row 2: *K2 with CC, P2 with MC, rep from *.

Rep rows 1 and 2 for patt.

Back

Back and front pieces are knit from side to side in St st.

With larger needles, CO 96 (112, 120, 120, 128, 128) sts. Beg neutral chart for sample A (page 44), and vibrant chart for sample B (page 44), and work until piece measures 18½ (21½, 23¼, 24¾, 27¾, 29½)" from beg. BO all sts.

Front

Work as for back until piece measures 6¼ (7½, 8, 8½, 10, 10¾)" ending with WS row.

Shape neck

Row 1: BO 1 st, finish row.

Row 2: Work to last 3 sts, P2tog, P1.

Rep last 2 rows until 7 (7, 7, 8, 8, 8) sts have been dec.

Work even for 13 (16, 18, 18, 20, 20) rows, ending with WS row.

Row 1: K1, M1, finish row.

Row 2: Work to last 2 sts, M1, P1.

Rep last 2 rows until 96 (112, 120, 120, 128, 128) sts are on needle.

Work even until piece measures 18½ (21½, 23¼, 24¾, 27¾, 29½)" from beg. BO all sts.

Sleeves (make 2)

With smaller needles and MC, CO 32 (40, 40, 48, 48, 56) sts. For sample A, work corrugated ribbing for 2½". For sample B, work K1, P1 ribbing for 2½" ending with WS row. On last row of ribbing, inc 8 (4, 6, 4, 8, 6) sts evenly spaced. Change to larger needles and following appropriate chart, inc 1 st at each side EOR 12 (15, 20, 19, 24, 25) times, every 4 rows 10 (10, 8, 9, 7, 8) times—84 (94, 102, 108, 118, 128) sts. Work even until piece measures 16½ (17½, 18, 18½, 19, 20)" from beg. BO all sts.

Finishing

Sew shoulder seams.

Collar: With circular needle or dpn and MC, starting at center front, PU 7 (9, 10, 10, 12, 12) sts from front, 15 (15, 15, 17, 17, 17) sts from right neck edge, 30 (32, 34, 36, 40, 40) sts across back neck, 15 (15, 15, 17, 17, 17) sts from left neck edge, and 7 (9, 10, 10, 12, 12) front neck sts. Join into rnd. Work 4 rnds in K1, P1 ribbing. On next rnd, beg working back and forth in K1, P1 ribbing and cont for another 3". BO all sts loosely in ribbing.

Bottom bands: With smaller needles and MC, PU 80 (92, 100, 108, 120, 128) sts across bottom edge of front. For sample A, work corrugated ribbing patt for 3". For sample B, work K1, P1 ribbing for 3". BO all sts loosely in ribbing. Rep across bottom edge of back.

Sew sleeves to body, sew sleeve and side seams. Weave in all ends and block as desired.

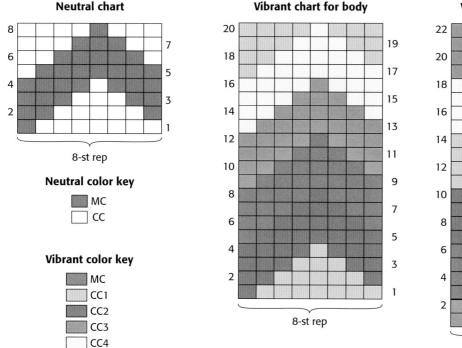

Neutral chart

8-st rep

Neutral color key
- MC
- CC

Vibrant color key
- MC
- CC1
- CC2
- CC3
- CC4

Vibrant chart for body

8-st rep

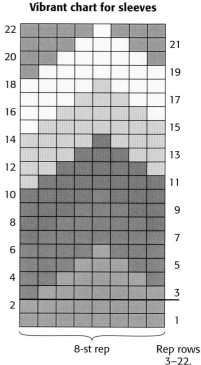

Vibrant chart for sleeves

8-st rep

Rep rows 3–22.

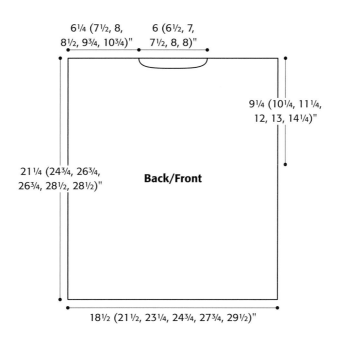

6¼ (7½, 8, 8½, 9¾, 10¾)"   6 (6½, 7, 7½, 8, 8)"

9¼ (10¼, 11¼, 12, 13, 14¼)"

21¼ (24¾, 26¾, 26¾, 28½, 28½)"

Back/Front

18½ (21½, 23¼, 24¾, 27¾, 29½)"

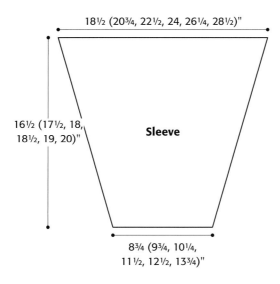

18½ (20¾, 22½, 24, 26¼, 28½)"

16½ (17½, 18, 18½, 19, 20)"

Sleeve

8¾ (9¾, 10¼, 11½, 12½, 13¾)"

Vests, Tunics, and Camisoles

Pattie Tunic

This soft, comforting sweater is
like wrapping yourself in fog
or a sunbeam.

Sample A

Sample B

Yarn Notes: This lace-weight yarn is almost more of a thread than a yarn. Both of these sweaters were stitched with needles that are larger than what this yarn weight usually calls for. Using large needles creates an open, lightweight fabric. The yarn is a blend—alpaca adds softness and warmth for comfort, and silk adds shine for style.

Materials

Shimmer from Knit Picks (70% baby alpaca, 30% silk; 50 g; 440 yds) **1**

Sample A

3 (3, 4, 5, 5, 6, 6) skeins • color E849 Morning Mist

Sample B

3 (3, 4, 5, 5, 6, 6) skeins • color E844 Happy Dance

Size 5 needles or size required to obtain gauge

Size 5 circular needle (24")

Size F (3.75mm) crochet hook

Gauge

16 sts and 26 rows = 4" in St st

Back

Using provisional CO (page 12), CO 79 (84, 98, 108, 118, 128, 137) sts. Work 2 (4, 4, 4, 4, 4, 2) rows in St st. Dec 1 st at each side of next row, then every 34 (24, 26, 26, 20, 20, 16) rows 2 (3, 3, 3, 4, 4, 5) times—73 (76, 90, 100, 108, 118, 125) sts. Work even in St st until piece measures 14¾ (15¾, 17, 17, 17¼, 17¼, 17¼)".

Shape armhole: BO 3 (3, 4, 5, 5, 6, 6) sts at beg of next 2 rows. Dec 1 st at each side EOR 4 (5, 9, 10, 12, 14, 16) times—59 (60, 64, 70, 74, 78, 81) sts. Work even until armhole measures 8½ (9, 9½, 10¼, 10½, 10¾, 11)".

Shape shoulders: BO 5 sts at beg of next 2 (2, 2, 0, 0, 0, 0) rows. BO 6 sts at beg of next 4 (4, 4, 2, 2, 0, 0) rows. BO 7 sts at beg of next 0 (0, 0, 4, 4, 6, 4) rows. BO 8 sts at beg of next 0 (0, 0, 0, 0, 0, 2) rows. Place rem 25 (26, 30, 30, 34, 36, 37) sts on holder.

Front

Work as for back to armhole. Work armhole shaping as for back, and AT SAME TIME beg neck shaping when 67 (70, 82, 90, 98, 106, 113) sts rem.

Shape neck: Work across 32 (34, 39, 44, 47, 51, 54) sts, join second ball of yarn and BO center 3 (2, 4, 2, 4, 4, 5) sts, finish row. Working both sides at same time, dec 1 st at each neck edge on next row, every 4 rows 0 (1, 2, 3, 6, 9, 7) times, every 5 rows 9 (10, 10, 10, 8, 6, 8) times, then every 6 rows 1 (0, 0, 0, 0, 0, 0) time—17 (17, 17, 20, 20, 21, 22) sts each side. Work even until armhole measures 8½ (9, 9½, 10¼, 10½, 10¾, 11)". Work shoulder shaping as for back.

Sleeves (make 2)

Using provisional CO, CO 86 (90, 101, 108, 115, 122, 128) sts. Working in St st, dec 1 st at each side of every 4 rows 0 (0, 0, 0, 0, 0, 4) times, every 5 rows 0 (0, 0, 0, 7, 13, 16) times, every 6 rows 0 (0, 4, 11, 10, 5, 0) times, every 7 rows 5 (13, 10, 4, 0, 0, 0) times, then every 8 rows 7 (0, 0, 0, 0, 0, 0) times—62 (64, 73, 78, 81, 86, 88) sts. Work even until piece measures 14¾ (15, 15¼, 15¼, 15¼, 15¼, 15¼)".

Shape cap: BO 3 (3, 4, 5, 5, 6, 6) sts at beg of next 2 rows. Dec 1 st at each side every row 5 (5, 7, 6, 7, 8, 8) times, EOR 10 (11, 9, 12, 11, 11, 11) times, then every row 5 (5, 7, 6, 7, 8, 8) times. BO rem 16 (16, 19, 20, 21, 20, 22) sts.

Finishing

Inc row: K1, *YO, K1, rep from *.

Bottom edge: PU 79 (84, 98, 108, 118, 128, 137) sts from provisional CO for back. Starting with RS row, work inc row. Work 7 rows even. Work inc row. Work 3 rows even. Purl 2 rows. BO all sts loosely. Rep on front.

Sleeve edge: PU 86 (90, 101, 108, 115, 122, 128) sts from provisional CO for sleeve. Starting with RS row, work inc row. Work 5 rows even. Work inc row. Purl 3 rows, BO loosely. Rep on second sleeve.

Sew one shoulder seam. With circular needle, PU 100 (102, 116, 122, 128, 132, 134) sts around neck edge, including sts on holders. Work inc row. Work 5 rows even. Work inc row. Purl 3 rows. BO all sts loosely. Sew rem shoulder and neck ruffle. Sew sleeves to body, sew sleeve and side seams. Weave in all ends and block as desired. Tack ruffle to body in several places to keep ruffle in place, if desired.

Bell-shaped sleeves, an A-line shape, and ruffles make this design ultrafeminine.

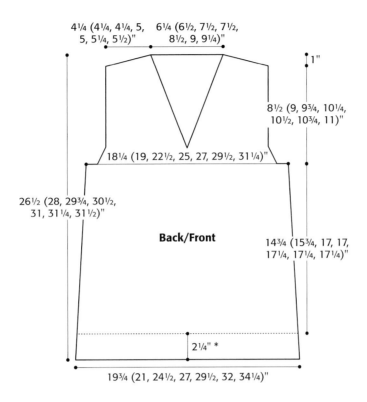

4¼ (4¼, 4¼, 5, 5, 5¼, 5½)"

6¼ (6½, 7½, 7½, 8½, 9, 9¼)"

1"

8½ (9, 9¾, 10¼, 10½, 10¾, 11)"

18¼ (19, 22½, 25, 27, 29½, 31¼)"

26½ (28, 29¾, 30½, 31, 31¼, 31½)"

Back/Front

14¾ (15¾, 17, 17, 17¼, 17¼, 17¼)"

2¼" *

19¾ (21, 24½, 27, 29½, 32, 34¼)"

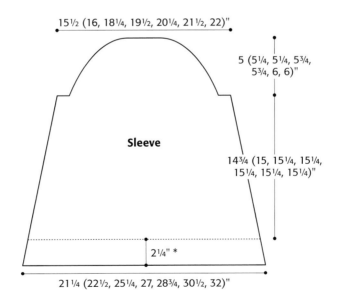

15½ (16, 18¼, 19½, 20¼, 21½, 22)"

5 (5¼, 5¼, 5¾, 5¾, 6, 6)"

Sleeve

14¾ (15, 15¼, 15¼, 15¼, 15¼, 15¼)"

2¼" *

21¼ (22½, 25¼, 27, 28¾, 30½, 32)"

* Bottom edges added after back, front, and sleeve pieces are completed.

Edna Vest

The royal quilting pattern on the front of this vest makes the most of a small amount of an expensive luxury yarn, or provides subtle interest to a workday basic.

Sample A

Sample B

Yarn Notes: Red and black provide visual and physical warmth, while shades of brown and beige offer a more neutral option. Cashmere may not fit into everyone's yarn budget, but the neutral version in acrylic and wool makes just as fashionable a statement.

Materials

Sample A

Royal Cashmere from Plymouth Yarn Company (100% cashmere; 50 g; 154 yds) (4)

MC 5 (5, 6, 7, 8, 9, 10) skeins • color 8062

CC 2 (2, 2, 2, 3, 3, 3) skeins • color 8010

Sample B

Wool-Ease from Lion Brand Yarn (20% wool, 80% acrylic; 3 oz; 197 yds) (4)

MC 4 (4, 5, 5, 6, 7, 7) skeins • color 126 Chocolate Brown

CC 1 (2, 2, 2, 2, 3, 3) skeins • color 402 Wheat

Size 8 needles or size required to obtain gauge

Size 6 needles or size required to obtain gauge

Size 6 circular needle (16")

Stitch marker

Stitch holders

Gauge

19 sts and 36 rows = 4" in royal quilting patt st on larger needles

18 sts and 24 rows = 4" in St st on smaller needles

Royal Quilting Pattern

(multiple of 6 + 3)

Row 1 (WS): With CC, K1, P1, *sl 5 wyib, P1, rep from * to last st, K1.

Row 2: With MC, knit.

Row 3: With MC, K1, purl to last st, K1.

Row 4: With CC, K1, sl 3 wyib, *sl right-hand needle from front to back under loose strand from row 1 and knit next st on left needle, bringing new st under strand to catch loose strand behind st, sl 5 wyib, rep from * to last 5 sts, knit next st under loose strand, sl 3 wyib, K1.

Row 5: With CC, K1, sl 3 wyib, *P1, sl 5 wyib, rep from * to last 5 sts, P1, sl 3 wyib, K1.

Row 6: With MC, knit.

Row 7: With MC, K1, purl to last st, K1.

Row 8: With CC, K1, *knit next st under loose strand from row 5, sl 5 wyib, rep from * to last 2 sts, knit next st under loose strand, K1.

Rep rows 1–8 for patt.

Twisted Ribbing for Back and Front

(worked back and forth)

(multiple of 2 + 1)

Row 1: *K1tbl, P1, rep from * to last st, K1tbl.

Row 2: *P1tbl, K1, rep from * to last st, P1tbl.

Rep rows 1–2 for patt.

Twisted Ribbing for Neckband and Armbands

(worked in the round)

(multiple of 2)

Rnd 1: *K1tbl, P1, rep from *.

Rep rnd 1 for patt.

Back

With smaller needles and MC, use tubular CO (page 15) to CO 73 (79, 89, 99, 109, 125, 129) sts. Work 3" in twisted ribbing for back and front. On last row of ribbing, inc 9 (9, 10, 11, 13, 14, 16) sts evenly spaced—82 (88, 99, 110, 122, 139, 145) sts.

Work in St st until piece measures 14½ (14½, 15½, 16, 16½, 16½, 16½)" from beg.

Shape armhole: BO 5 (7, 9, 13, 16, 24, 26) sts at beg of next 2 rows—72 (74, 81, 84, 90, 91, 93) sts. Cont in St st until piece measures 23 (23½, 25, 26½, 27½, 29½, 30)" from beg.

Shape neck: On next row, work across 23 (23, 25, 25, 28, 28, 28) sts, place center 26 (28, 31, 34, 34, 35, 37) sts on holder, join second ball of yarn and finish row. Working both sides at same time, BO 1 st at each neck edge. Cont in St st until piece measures 23½ (24, 25½, 27, 28, 30, 30½)" from beg. BO 22 (22, 24, 24, 27, 27, 27) sts across each shoulder.

Front

With smaller needles and MC, use tubular CO to CO 77 (83, 93, 105, 115, 131, 137) sts. Work 3" in twisted ribbing for back and front. On last row of ribbing, inc 10 (10, 12, 12, 14, 16, 16) sts evenly spaced—87 (93, 105, 117, 129, 147, 153) sts. Change to larger needles and beg royal quilting patt. Work in patt until piece measures 14½ (14½, 15½, 16, 16½, 16½, 16½)" from beg. Work armhole and neck shaping at same time.

Shape armhole and neck: BO 7 (7, 10, 16, 20, 28, 31) sts at beg of next row. On next row, work across 36 (39, 42, 42, 44, 45, 45) sts, place center st on a holder (or a safety pin), join second ball of yarn and finish row. BO 7 (7, 10, 16, 20, 28, 31) sts at beg of next row—36 (39, 42, 42, 44, 45, 45) sts each shoulder. Work neck decs as follows: knit to 3 sts before neck edge, K2tog, K1. On second side, K1, ssk, knit to end. Working both sides at same time, dec 1 st at each neck edge every 4 rows 6 (7, 11, 18, 9, 3, 2) times, then every 6 rows 8 (8, 6, 0, 10, 17, 18) times—22 (24, 25, 24, 25, 25, 25) sts each shoulder. Work even in patt until piece measures 23½ (24, 25½, 27, 28, 30, 30½)" from beg ending with row 4 or 8. Slide sts back to left-hand needle, and BO all shoulder sts with MC.

Finishing

Sew shoulder and side seams.

Armbands: With circular needle and MC, PU 94 (100, 108, 126, 138, 172, 180) sts around left armhole. Join and pm to indicate beg of rnd. Work 8 rnds in twisted ribbing for neckband and armbands. BO all sts with tubular BO (page 15). Rep on right armhole.

Neckband: With circular needle and MC, PU 26 (28, 31, 33, 34, 35, 37) sts from back neck holder, 54 (58, 60, 66, 70, 82, 84) sts from left front neck edge, pm, center st from holder, 54 (58, 60, 66, 70, 82, 84) sts from right front edge, pm to indicate end of rnd—135 (145, 152, 166, 175, 200, 206) sts. Join and pm to indicate beg of rnd. **Next rnd:** Work in twisted ribbing for neckband and armbands to 2 sts before center marker, sl next st, K1, psso, sl marker, K1, K2tog, finish row in twisted ribbing. Rep last rnd 8 times. BO all sts with tubular BO (page 15).

Weave in all ends and block as desired.

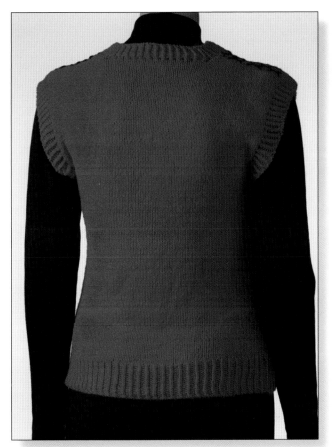

A plain back keeps the focus on the front and speeds up your knitting.

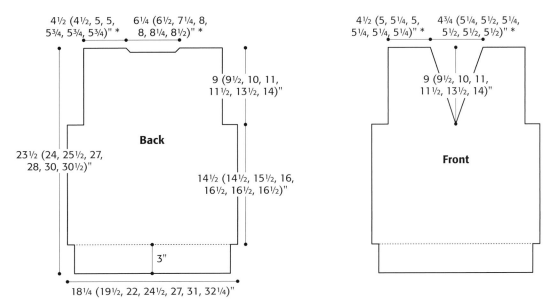

4½ (4½, 5, 5, 5¾, 5¾, 5¾)" *

6¼ (6½, 7¼, 8, 8, 8¼, 8½)" *

4½ (5, 5¼, 5, 5¼, 5¼, 5¼)" *

4¾ (5¼, 5½, 5¼, 5½, 5½, 5½)" *

9 (9½, 10, 11, 11½, 13½, 14)"

9 (9½, 10, 11, 11½, 13½, 14)"

Back

Front

23½ (24, 25½, 27, 28, 30, 30½)"

14½ (14½, 15½, 16, 16½, 16½, 16½)"

3"

18¼ (19½, 22, 24½, 27, 31, 32¼)"

* Measurements are slightly different on the front and the back due to a slight difference in gauge on the front and the back. Ease the shoulders together when sewing.

Rose Camisole

Here's a swingy summer top,
perfect with jeans or a skirt, that can
be worn with either side out.

Sample A

Sample B

Size: Extra Small (Small, Medium, Large, 1X, 2X, 3X)

Finished Measurements:
Bust: 33 (35, 39, 43, 47, 51, 55)"
Length: 14 (14½, 14¾, 15¼, 15½, 15½, 15½)"
without straps

Yarn Notes: This yarn, although primarily cotton, is not as heavy as most cottons because of the addition of polyamide. This blending also makes the yarn springier and more elastic than all-cotton yarn. The thicker yarn makes this quick to knit—just the thing for a summer afternoon.

Materials

Cotton Rich from Cascade Yarns (64% cotton, 36% polyamide; 50 g; 80 yds) (4)

Sample A

4 (4, 5, 5, 5, 6, 6) skeins • color 2625

Sample B

4 (4, 5, 5, 5, 6, 6) skeins • color 3131

Size 7 circular needle (24") or size required to obtain gauge

Size I (5.5 mm) crochet hook

Gauge

16 sts and 20 rows = 4" in patt st

Rose Lace Pattern

(multiple of 4 + 3 + 2 edge sts)

Rnd 1: K3, *YO, K2tog, K2, rep from * to last 6 sts before marker, YO, K2tog, K4.

Rnd 2: K3, *K1, YO, K2tog, K1, rep from * to last 6 sts before marker, K1, YO, K2tog, K3.

Rnd 3: K1, YO, K2tog, *K2, YO, K2tog, rep from * to last 6 sts before marker, K2, YO, K2tog, K2.

Rnd 4: K2, YO, *K2tog, K2, YO, rep from * to last 6 sts before marker, K2tog, K2, YO, K2tog, K1.

Rnd 5: K3, *K1, ssk, YO, K1, rep from * to last 6 sts before marker, K1, ssk, YO, K3.

Rnd 6: K3, *ssk, YO, K2, rep from * to last 6 sts before marker, ssk, YO, K4.

Rnd 7: K2, ssk, *YO, K2, ssk, rep from * to last 6 sts before marker, YO, K2, ssk, YO, K1.

Rnd 8: K1, ssk, YO, *K2, ssk, YO, rep from * to last 6 sts before marker, K2, ssk, YO, K2.

Rep rnds 1–8 for patt.

This garment is worked in the round, but you will begin the directions for each round from the beginning after each marker. For example, work round 1, including beginning stitches, required repeats, and ending stitches to the next marker. Slip the marker and begin round 1 again working to the next marker. Then work round 2, working the round from the beginning after each marker. Continue this way through all the rounds to the desired measurement.

Body

CO 66 (70, 78, 86, 94, 102, 110) sts, pm, CO 66 (70, 78, 86, 94, 102, 110) sts, pm. Join sts into rnd, being careful not to twist. Use a different-colored marker to indicate the beg of the rnd. Beg Rose lace patt and work to first marker, sl marker, and work same rnd to the next marker which is the beg-of-rnd marker. Beg rnd 2, and work 8-row patt for 40 rows (8") for all sizes. Change to St st and work until piece measures 14 (14½, 14¾, 15¼, 15½, 15½, 15½)" from beg. BO all sts between markers on 1 side. Work front on rem sts.

Front: BO 4 (3, 5, 6, 6, 6, 7) sts at beg of next 2 rows. Dec 1 st at each side of EOR 6 (8, 9, 10, 13, 15, 17) times and AT SAME TIME shape neck when 50 (58, 58, 64, 72, 82, 86) sts rem.

Shape neck: Work across 5 (7, 7, 8, 11, 15, 15) sts, join second ball of yarn and BO 40 (44, 44, 48, 50, 52, 56) sts, finish row. Working both sides at same time, BO 1 st at side edge EOR until 3 sts rem, then cont on rem 3 sts until strap is long enough to go over the top of the shoulder and reach the top of the back piece (see "Strap Options," below). Sew sides and try top on before binding off sts.

STRAP OPTIONS

Depending on your own shape and the look you want, you can crisscross the straps on the back, or tie them around the neck to form a halter. You could also use ribbon in place of knitted straps. To do this, simply BO all front stitches at once and sew on ribbons.

Finishing

Decide which side you want to be the RS—both look good, but different. Sew straps as desired. With crochet hook, and with RS facing you, work a row of sc (page 13) around neck and armholes, including straps and bottom edge.

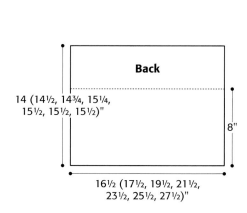

Back

14 (14½, 14¾, 15¼, 15½, 15½, 15½)"

8"

16½ (17½, 19½, 21½, 23½, 25½, 27½)"

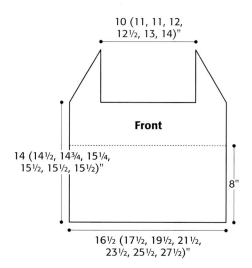

10 (11, 11, 12, 12½, 13, 14)"

Front

14 (14½, 14¾, 15¼, 15½, 15½, 15½)"

8"

16½ (17½, 19½, 21½, 23½, 25½, 27½)"

Wear the camisole with this side showing . . .

. . . or turn it inside out to display the heavier zigzags on the other side.

Cecile Vest

Sample A

The shaping and finishing of this vest are kept simple to keep the emphasis on the cable pattern.

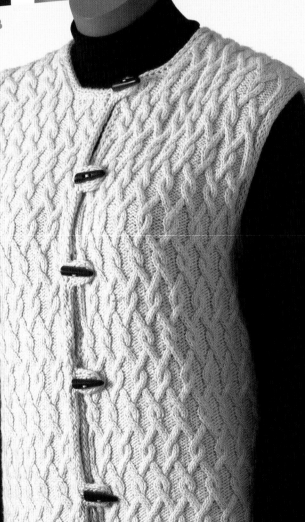

Sample B

Yarn Notes: This yarn offers the warmth of wool with the sheen of silk. In the vibrant version, the fibers absorb color to allow rich dyeing with subtle variations. The natural shades of the neutral version offer versatile pairing with many outfits. Either version is a soft and warm showplace for your cables.

Materials

Synchronicity from Alchemy Yarns of Transformation (50% wool, 50% silk; 50 g; 110 yds) (4)

Sample A

12 (13, 14, 17, 19, 20, 23) skeins • color 17E Tennessee Green

Sample B

12 (13, 14, 17, 19, 20, 23) skeins • color 26A Empty Sky

Size 6 needles or size needed to obtain gauge

Size 5 needles

Cable needle

Sewing needle and thread

Buttons:

  Sample A: 7 buttons, ¾" diameter

  Sample B: 7 toggles, 1½" long

Gauge

28 sts and 30 rows = 4" in cable patt on larger needles

Cable Pattern

Chart on page 63
(multiple of 8)

T3F: Sl next 2 sts to cn, hold in front, P1, K2 from cn.

T3B: Sl next st to cn, hold to back, K2, P1 from cn.

C4B: Sl next 2 sts to cn, hold in back, K2, K2 from cn.

C4F: Sl next 2 sts to cn, hold in front, K2, K2 from cn.

Foundation row (WS): K1, *P2, K2, rep from * to last 3 sts, P2, K1.

Row 1: P1, *T3F, T3B, P2, rep from * to last 7 sts, T3F, T3B, P1.

Row 2: K2, *P4, K4, rep from * to last 6 sts, P4, K2.

Row 3: P2, *C4F, P4, rep from * to last 6 sts, C4F, P2.

Row 4: Rep row 2.

Row 5: P1, * T3B, T3F, P2, rep from * to last 7 sts, T3B, T3F, P1.

Row 6: K1, *P2, K2, rep from * to last 3 sts, P2, K1.

Rows 7–12: Rep rows 1–6.

Row 13: *T3B, P2, T3F, rep from *.

Row 14: P2, *K4, P4, rep from * to last 6 sts, K4, P2.

Row 15: K2, *P4, C4B, rep from * to last 6 sts, P4, K2.

Row 16: Rep row 14.

Row 17: K2, P3, *T3B, T3F, P2, rep from * to last 3 sts, P1, K2.

Row 18: P2, K3, *P2, K2, rep from * to last 3 sts, K1, P2.

Row 19: K2, P3, *T3F, T3B, P2, rep from * to last 3 sts, P1, K2.

Row 20: Rep row 14.

Row 21: Rep row 15.

Row 22: Rep row 14.

Row 23: *T3F, P2, T3B, rep from *.

Row 24: Rep row 6.

Rep rows 1–24 for patt.

Back

With larger needles, CO 136 (144, 152, 168, 184, 192, 208) sts. Work in cable patt until piece measures 14 (14½, 15, 15½, 16, 16, 16)" from beg.

Shape armholes: BO 10 (7, 8, 12, 13, 10, 11) sts at beg of next 2 rows—116 (130, 136, 144, 158, 172, 186) sts. Work even until piece measures 22½ (23½, 24, 25½, 26½, 27½, 28½)" from beg.

Shape neck: Work across 38 (43, 46, 48, 54, 59, 66) sts, join second ball of yarn and BO center 40 (44, 44, 48, 50, 54, 54) sts, finish row. Working both sides at same time, on next row dec 1 st at neck edge. Work even until piece measures 23 (24, 24½, 26, 27, 28, 29)" from beg. BO 37 (42, 45, 47, 53, 58, 65) sts across each shoulder.

Fronts (make 2, Reversing Shaping)

With larger needle, CO 68 (72, 76, 84, 92, 96, 104) sts. Work as for back, starting with fifth st of patt for Extra Small, Medium, Large and 1X. Work armhole shaping to match back. Work even until piece measures 20 (21, 21½, 23, 23½, 24½, 25½) from beg.

Shape neck: At neck edge, BO 11 (14, 13, 15, 14, 16, 16) sts on next row. Dec 1 st at neck edge on EOR 10 (9, 10, 10, 12, 12, 12) times—37 (42, 45, 47, 53, 58, 65) sts. Work even until piece measures 23 (24, 24½, 26, 27, 28, 29)" from beg. BO all sts.

Finishing

Seam shoulders.

Armbands: With smaller needles, CO 4 sts, and work approx 18 (19, 19, 21, 22, 24, 26)" of I-cord (page 11). I-cord should reach around armhole when slightly stretched. Using yarn needle and yarn, sew I-cord around armhole. Rep on opposite side.

Front, neck, and bottom bands: Sew side seams. With smaller needles, CO 4 sts and work approx 100 (100, 110, 120, 130, 130, 140)" of I-cord. Place 7 markers evenly spaced along right front for button loops. Starting at lower right edge, sew I-cord slightly stretched along bottom front, across back, across left bottom front, up left front edge, around neck, and down right front including loops as follows: at each marker form a loop about 1" long, then resume sewing to next marker.

Weave in all ends and block as desired. Using sewing needle and thread, sew toggles or buttons opposite loops. If the loops are too big, st the edges of the loop together with yarn or thread to make the loop smaller.

Cable pattern

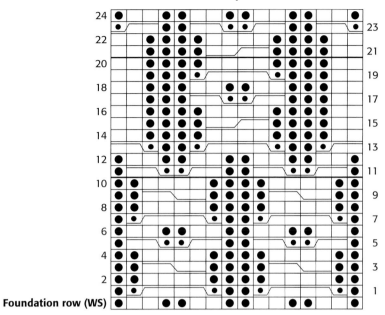

Foundation row (WS)

Stitch key

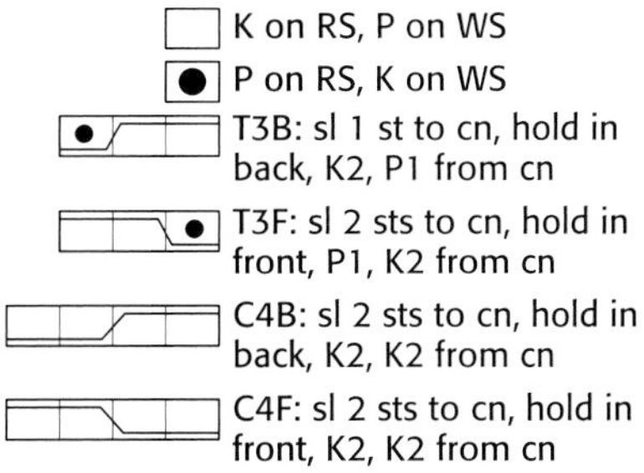

☐ K on RS, P on WS

● P on RS, K on WS

T3B: sl 1 st to cn, hold in back, K2, P1 from cn

T3F: sl 2 sts to cn, hold in front, P1, K2 from cn

C4B: sl 2 sts to cn, hold in back, K2, K2 from cn

C4F: sl 2 sts to cn, hold in front, K2, K2 from cn

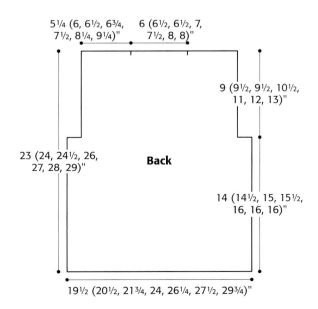

5¼ (6, 6½, 6¾, 7½, 8¼, 9¼)"

6 (6½, 6½, 7, 7½, 8, 8)"

9 (9½, 9½, 10½, 11, 12, 13)"

23 (24, 24½, 26, 27, 28, 29)"

Back

14 (14½, 15, 15½, 16, 16, 16)"

19½ (20½, 21¾, 24, 26¼, 27½, 29¾)"

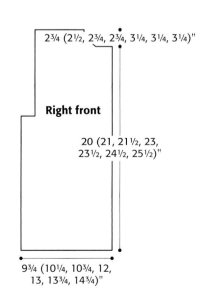

2¾ (2½, 2¾, 2¾, 3¼, 3¼, 3¼)"

Right front

20 (21, 21½, 23, 23½, 24½, 25½)"

9¾ (10¼, 10¾, 12, 13, 13¾, 14¾)"

Sue Tunic

Sample A

Sample B

Wear this tunic over a bathing suit
or camisole in the summer, then
over a turtleneck all winter.

Yarn Notes: This organic cotton, whether natural or dyed, is as soft as your favorite pair of old jeans. The openwork pattern keeps the cotton from becoming heavy while the simple design coordinates with many different styles.

Materials

Sample A

3 (4, 4, 5, 5, 6, 6) balls of Blue Sky Cotton from Blue Sky Alpacas (100% cotton; 100 g; 150 yds), color 618 Orchid (4)

Sample B

3 (4, 4, 5, 5, 6, 6) balls of Organic Cotton from Blue Sky Alpacas (100% cotton; 100 g; 150 yds), color 80 Bone (4)

Size 9 needles or size needed to obtain gauge

Stitch markers

Gauge

15¼ sts and 20 rows = 4" in lace patt

Lace Pattern

(multiple of 4 + 1)

Rows 1 and 3 (WS): Purl.

Row 2: K1, *YO, sl 2 sts as if to knit, K1, p2sso, YO, K1, rep from *.

Row 4: Ssk, YO, K1, *YO, sl 2 sts as if to knit, K1, p2sso, YO, K1, rep from * to last 2 sts, YO, K2tog.

Rep rows 1–4 for patt.

Back and Front (Make 2 the Same)

CO 73 (81, 85, 93, 97, 105, 113) sts. Work in lace patt until piece measures 19 (19, 19, 19½, 20, 20, 20)" from beg, pm at each side to indicate underarms. Work until piece measures 28 (28, 28½, 30, 31, 32, 33)" from beg. BO using "Sewn Bind Off" (page 13).

Sleeves (Make 2)

CO 37 (37, 37, 45, 49, 49, 53) sts. Beg lace patt, working inc into patt, inc 1 st at each side EOR 0 (0, 0, 0, 0, 0, 4) times, every 4 rows 10 (10, 12, 10, 9, 21, 19) times, then every 6 rows 6 (6, 5, 7, 8, 0, 0) times—69 (69, 71, 79, 83, 91, 99) sts. Work even until piece measures 16 (16¾, 16½, 17, 17½, 17½, 17½)" from beg. BO all sts.

Finishing

Tack edges of front and back together. Sew sleeves to body, sew side and sleeve seams. Try sweater on and mark (with pins or yarn scraps) where edges of neck opening should be, sew shoulders as desired. Work in all ends and block as desired.

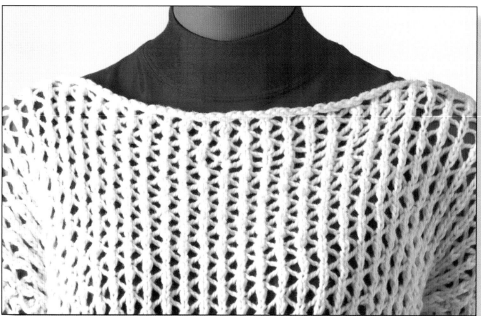

Make the neck opening as narrow or as wide as you like.

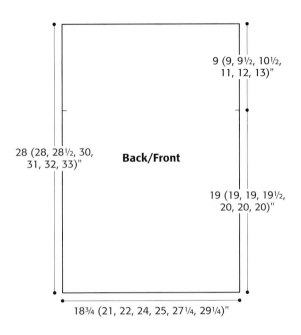

9 (9, 9½, 10½, 11, 12, 13)"

28 (28, 28½, 30, 31, 32, 33)"

Back/Front

19 (19, 19, 19½, 20, 20, 20)"

18¾ (21, 22, 24, 25, 27¼, 29¼)"

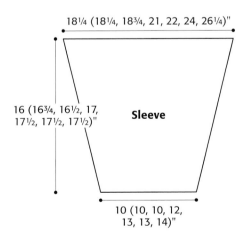

18¼ (18¼, 18¾, 21, 22, 24, 26¼)"

16 (16¾, 16½, 17, 17½, 17½, 17½)"

Sleeve

10 (10, 10, 12, 13, 13, 14)"

Cardigans and Jackets

Ruth Jacket

Sample A

Sample B

Create the look of a wrapped sweater without the bulk by using a false edge.

Yarn Notes: Color choice and combination make a real difference in this pair of sweaters. In the bolder version, colors with high levels of contrast make the color-work pattern really "pop." In the neutral version, colors of more similar intensities allow the pattern to show, but in a much more subtle way.

Materials

Lone Star from Alchemy Yarns of Transformation (55% mohair, 45% merino wool; 100 g; 145 yds) (4)

Sample A

MC 7 (7, 8, 9, 10, 11, 12) skeins • color 45S Koi Pond

CC 7 (7, 8, 9, 10, 11, 12) skeins • color 82W Janboy's Sapphire

Sample B

MC 7 (7, 8, 9, 10, 11, 12) skeins • color 65E Dragon

CC 7 (7, 8, 9, 10, 11, 12) skeins • color 60S San Francisco Sky

Size 8 needles or size required to obtain gauge

Size 6 straight needles and size 6 circular needle (24" or longer)

Stitch holders

Stitch markers

Gauge

20 sts and 20 rows = 4" in patt st on larger needles

Color Work Pattern

Chart on page 72
(multiple of 10)

Row 1 (RS): *K1 MC, K3 CC, K1 MC, K3 CC, K1 MC, K1 CC, rep from *.

Row 2: *P2 MC, P2 CC, P3 MC, P2 CC, P1 MC, rep from *.

Row 3: *K3 CC, K1 MC, K1 CC, K1 MC, K3 CC, K1 MC, rep from *.

Row 4: *P2 CC, P3 MC, P1 CC, P3 MC, P1 CC, rep from *.

Row 5: *K2 MC, K5 CC, K2 MC, K1 CC, rep from *.

Row 6: Rep row 4.

Row 7: Rep row 3.

Row 8: *P1 CC, P1 MC, P2 CC, P3 MC, P2 CC, P1 MC, rep from *.

Row 9: Rep row 1.

Row 10: *P1 CC, P3 MC, P3 CC, P3 MC, rep from *.

Row 11: *K2 CC, K2 MC, K1 CC, K2 MC, K3 CC, rep from *.

Row 12: Rep row 10.

Rep rows 1–12 for patt.

Back

With smaller needles and MC, CO 90 (100, 110, 120, 130, 140, 150) sts. Work 5 rows in St st ending with RS row. Change to larger needles and knit 1 row (this is the fold line). Working in St st, beg color work patt and cont until piece measures 14½ (14½, 15, 15½, 16, 16, 16)" from fold line, pm at each side to indicate underarms. Work even until piece measures 24 (24, 25, 26½, 27½, 28½, 29½)" from fold line. BO 27 (34, 37, 41, 45, 49, 54) sts at beg of next 2 rows. Place rem 36 (32, 36, 38, 40, 42, 42) sts on holder for back neck.

Front

Work as for back until piece measures 16 (14½, 15, 15½, 16, 16, 16)" from fold line. Work to center, join second ball of yarn of each color and finish row. Turn, and working both sides at same time, dec 1 st at neck edge every row 10 (0, 0, 0, 0, 0, 0) times, EOR 8 (11, 14, 13, 13, 14, 10) times, every 4 rows 0 (5, 4, 6, 7, 7, 11) times in the following manner: work to 3 sts before center divide, K2tog (on RS row) or P2tog (on WS row), work next st, work first st after central divide, ssk (on RS row) or ssp (on WS row), finish row in patt. Work even until piece measures 24 (24, 25, 26½, 27½, 28½, 29½)" from fold line. BO 26 (33, 36, 40, 44, 48, 53) sts across each shoulder.

Sleeves (Make 2)

With smaller needles and MC, CO 60 (60, 60, 60, 70, 70, 70) sts. Work 5 rows in St st, ending with RS row. Change to larger needles and knit 1 row (this is the fold line). Working in St st, beg color work patt and working inc into patt, inc 1 st on each side every 2 rows 0 (0, 0, 7, 8, 15, 24) times, every 4 rows 12 (12, 18, 18, 15, 13, 9) times, then every 6 rows 6 (6, 2, 0, 0, 0, 0) times—96 (96, 100, 110, 116, 126, 136) sts. Work until piece measures 17½ (17½, 17½, 18, 16, 17, 17½)" from fold line. BO all sts.

Finishing

Sew shoulder seams.

Front band and neckband: Using MC and circular needle, PU 31 (38, 39, 44, 47, 49, 55) sts from right neck edge, 36 (32, 36, 38, 40, 42, 42) sts from holder for back neck, and 31 (38, 39, 44, 47, 49, 55) sts from left front edge, cont picking up sts from body of sweater, moving over 1 st and down 1 row until you reach the edge of the body. Work back and forth in garter st for 6 rows, BO all sts loosely. Fold edges of sweater pieces at fold lines and sew hems to backs of pieces.

Sew sleeves to body, sew sleeve and side seams, catching edge of garter st band in side seam. Sew beg of garter st band to underside of front. Weave in all ends and block as desired.

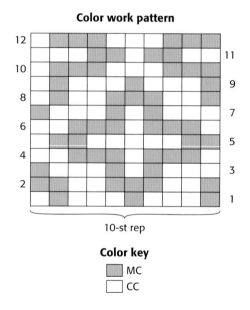

Color work pattern

10-st rep

Color key
- MC
- CC

The edging gives the illusion of two fronts being wrapped. The diagonal line provides a slimming effect.

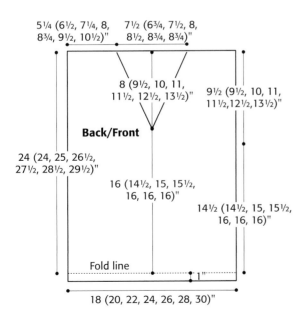

5¼ (6½, 7¼, 8, 8¾, 9½, 10½)"   7½ (6¾, 7½, 8, 8½, 8¾, 8¾)"

8 (9½, 10, 11, 11½, 12½, 13½)"   9½ (9½, 10, 11, 11½,12½,13½)"

Back/Front

24 (24, 25, 26½, 27½, 28½, 29½)"

16 (14½, 15, 15½, 16, 16, 16)"

14½ (14½, 15, 15½, 16, 16, 16)"

Fold line
1"
18 (20, 22, 24, 26, 28, 30)"

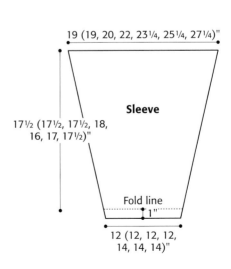

19 (19, 20, 22, 23¼, 25¼, 27¼)"

Sleeve

17½ (17½, 17½, 18, 16, 17, 17½)"

Fold line
1"
12 (12, 12, 12, 14, 14, 14)"

Jayne Cardigan

Sample A

This tunic-length sweater also works in a longer length as a light coat.

Sample B

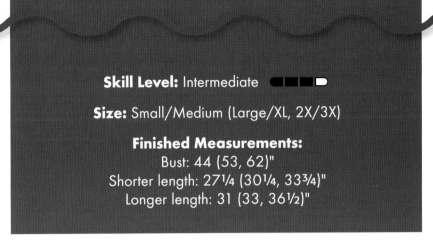

Yarn Notes: The hand-dyed yarn used in both versions of this sweater has subtle variations within each skein. This gives the finished pieces visual interest without distracting from the pattern of cables and lace. The blend of silk and merino wool is lightweight but warm, and the open stitch work prevents the design from becoming too heavy.

Materials

Silk and Merino Worsted from Cherry Tree Hill Yarns (50% silk, 50% merino; 4 oz; 278 yds) (4)

Sample A

8 (12, 14) skeins • color Pink

Sample B

7 (10, 12) skeins • color Black

Size 8 needles or size needed to obtain gauge

Cable needle

⅝"-diameter buttons:

> **Sample A:** 10 of JHB International, Hartford 49785

> **Sample B:** 8 of JHB International, Pembroke 94933

Size E (3.5 mm) crochet hook

Gauge

25½ sts and 35 rows = 4" in patt

Cable and Lace Pattern

Chart on page 77
(multiple of 14 + 1)

C6B: Sl next 3 sts to cn and hold at back, K3, K3 from cn.

C6F: Sl next 3 sts on cn and hold at front, K3, K3 from cn.

Rows 1, 3, 5, and 7 (WS): K1, *P2tog, YO, P11, K1, rep from *.

Row 2: K1, *ssk, YO, C6B, K6, rep from *.

Row 4: K1, *ssk, YO, K12, rep from *.

Row 6: K1, *ssk, YO, K3, C6F, K3, rep from *.

Row 8: Rep row 4.

Rep rows 1–8 for patt.

Back

CO 141 (169, 197) sts. Work in cable and lace patt until piece measures 18½ (20, 20)" for short version or 22¼ (22¾, 22¾)" for long version from beg.

Shape armhole: BO 14 (17, 21) sts at beg of next 2 rows. Dec 1 st at each side EOR 13 (16, 21) times—87 (103, 113) sts. Work even in patt until piece measures 26½ (29½, 33)" for short version or 30¼ (32¼, 35¾)" for long version from beg.

Shape shoulders: BO 7 (9, 10) sts at beg of next 2 rows. BO 8 (9, 10) sts at beg of next 4 rows. BO rem 41 (49, 53) sts.

Fronts (Make 2, Reversing Shaping)

CO 71 (85, 99) sts. Work as for back, including armhole shaping, and AT SAME TIME beg neck shaping when piece measures 19¼ (20¾, 20¾)" for short version or 22 (23½, 23½)" for long version from beg.

Shape neck: Dec 1 st at neck edge EOR 13 (14, 2) times, then every 4 rows 7 (10, 24) times—24 (28, 31) sts. Work even in patt until piece measures 26½ (29½, 33)" for short version or 30¼ (32¼, 35¾)" for long version from beg.

Shape shoulders: Work shoulders as for back.

Sleeves

CO 57 (71, 85) sts. Beg cable and lace patt, and inc 1 st at each side EOR 0 (0, 13) times, every 4 rows 2 (0, 29) times, every 6 rows 22 (17, 0) times, then every 8 rows 0 (5, 0) times—105 (115, 169) sts. Work even in patt until piece measures 16¾ (17, 17)" from beg.

Shape cap: BO 14 (15, 21) sts at beg of next 2 rows. Dec 1 st at each side EOR 13 (14, 21) times, every row 2 (5, 1) times, then EOR 6 (6, 13) times. BO 4 (4, 7) sts at beg of next 4 rows. BO rem 19 (19, 29) sts.

Finishing

Sew shoulder seams. Sew sleeves to body, sew side and sleeve seams. Use crochet hook to work 1 row of sc around the body edge and sleeve edges. Sew buttons spaced evenly along left front, aligning each one with a hole in the lace. Weave in all ends and block as desired.

The lace pattern of the cardigan forms its own buttonholes.

Cable and lace pattern

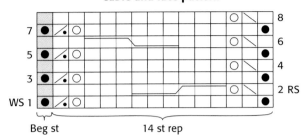

Beg st   14 st rep

Stitch key

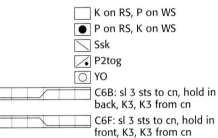

☐ K on RS, P on WS

● P on RS, K on WS

◻ Ssk

◿ P2tog

◯ YO

C6B: sl 3 sts to cn, hold in back, K3, K3 from cn

C6F: sl 3 sts to cn, hold in front, K3, K3 from cn

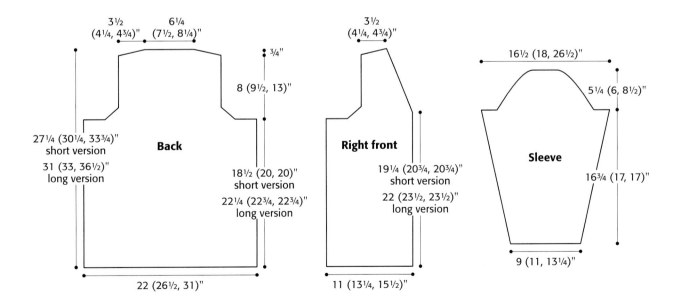

Back

3½ (4¼, 4¾)" 6¼ (7½, 8¼)"

¾"

8 (9½, 13)"

27¼ (30¼, 33¾)" short version

31 (33, 36½)" long version

18½ (20, 20)" short version

22¼ (22¾, 22¾)" long version

22 (26½, 31)"

Right front

3½ (4¼, 4¾)"

19¼ (20¾, 20¾)" short version

22 (23½, 23½)" long version

11 (13¼, 15½)"

Sleeve

16½ (18, 26½)"

5¼ (6, 8½)"

16¾ (17, 17)"

9 (11, 13¼)"

Alice Jacket

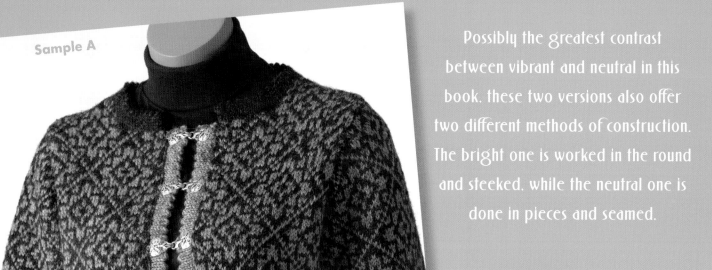

Sample A

Possibly the greatest contrast between vibrant and neutral in this book, these two versions also offer two different methods of construction. The bright one is worked in the round and steeked, while the neutral one is done in pieces and seamed.

Sample B

Skill Level: Experienced ◼◼◼◼

Size: Extra Small/Small (Medium/Large, 1X, 2X/3X)

Finished Measurements:
Bust: 40 (48, 56, 64)"
Length: 21 (23, 25½, 28½)"

Yarn Notes: You can see how color choice dramatically changes the look of this piece. The neutral version could easily fit into a quiet wardrobe while the almost-neon version really "pops." Or you could consider the middle ground, and knit up a version of your own that incorporates some bright and some subdued colors (in whatever proportions work best for you).

Materials

Sample A

Heilo from Dale of Norway (100% wool; 1¾ oz; 109 yds) (2)

MC 7 (9, 11, 15) balls • color 0083

CC1 5 (7, 9, 11) balls • color 0007

CC2 1 (1, 2, 2) ball • color 0004

CC3 1 (1, 1, 1) ball • color 3918

Sample B

Falk from Dale of Norway (100% wool; 1¾ oz; 116 yds) (2)

MC 7 (9, 11, 15) balls • color 0144

CC1 5 (7, 9, 11) balls • color 0184

CC2 1 (1, 2, 2) ball • color 6027

CC3 1 (1, 1, 1) ball • color 0120

Size 4 needles or size required to obtain gauge (24" circular needle for sample B)

Size 3 needles

Stitch markers

6 pairs of clasps

Tapestry needle

Gauge

24 sts and 24 rows = 4" in patt st on larger needles

Picot Row

K1, *YO, K2tog, rep from * to last st, YO, K1.

SAMPLE A

This sweater is knit in pieces and sewn together.

Back

With smaller needles and MC, CO 120 (144, 168, 192) sts. Work 6 rows in St st. Work picot row. Change to larger needles and work 5 rows in St st. Cont in St st, beg chart A (page 82), rep rows 30–53 as necessary. Cont until piece measures 12 (13, 13½, 13½)" from picot row.

Shape armholes: BO 10 (14, 16, 20) sts at beg of next 2 rows. Dec 1 st at each side EOR 10 (13, 16, 19) times—80 (90, 104, 114) sts. Work even in patt until piece measures 20 (22, 24½, 27½)" from picot row.

Shape shoulders: BO 7 (8, 9, 11) sts at beg of next 2 rows. Work across 15 (17, 19, 21) sts, join a second ball of yarn of each color, BO 36 (40, 48, 50) sts for back neck, finish row. Working both sides at same time, BO 7 (8, 9, 10) sts at beg of next row and dec 1 st at neck edge. BO 7 (8, 9, 10) sts at beg of next 3 rows.

Fronts (Make 2, Reversing Shaping)

With smaller needles and MC, CO 60 (72, 84, 96) sts. Work as for back, including armhole shaping—40 (45, 52, 57) sts.

> For Extra Small/Small and 1X, you will work 2½ and 3½ rep of patt on each side of front. To line up patt correctly, start right side with first st of patt, and start left side with st 13 of chart A.

Work until piece measures 19 (21, 23, 24½)" from picot row.

Shape neck: At neck edge, BO 14 (16, 18, 15) sts. Dec 1 st at neck edge EOR 5 (5, 7, 11) times—21 (24, 27, 31) sts. Work until piece measures 20 (22, 24½, 27½)" from picot row, work shoulder shaping as for back.

Sleeves (Make 2)

With smaller needles and MC, CO 50 (58, 72, 78) sts. Work 6 rows in St st. Work picot row. Change to larger needles and work 5 rows in St st. Cont in St st, beg chart A on st 23 (20, 1, 22), and rep rows 30–53 of chart as necessary. Working incs into patt, inc 1 st at each side EOR 0 (6, 12, 39) times, every 4 rows 21 (19, 18, 6) times, then every 6 rows 2 (0, 0, 0) times—96 (108, 132, 168) sts. Work even in patt until piece measures 14¼ (15½, 17, 18)".

Shape cap: BO 10 (14, 16, 20) at beg of next 2 rows. Dec 1 st at each side EOR 10 (13, 16, 19) times, then every row 5 (3, 5, 11) times. BO 4 (4, 5, 7) sts at beg of next 4 rows. BO rem 30 (32, 38, 40) sts.

SAMPLE B

This sweater is knit in the round with steeks (page 14).

Body

With smaller needles and MC, CO 240 (288, 336, 384) sts, pm after 60 (72, 84, 96) sts, then after next 120 (144, 168, 192) sts. Work 6 rows in St st. Work picot row. Change to larger needles and knit 5 rows. Beg chart B on page 83. Pm at end of rnd 1, CO 4 sts for steek, pm. Join and work chart in the round, rep rows 30–53 as necessary. The 4 steek sts are not part of chart. Work them in whatever color you are carrying when you come to them, alternating the two colors to avoid a long float of one color. Remember these 4 sts will be cut away so the color sequence doesn't matter. Work until piece measures 12 (13, 13½, 13½)" from picot row.

Shape armhole: BO 10 (14, 16, 20) sts before and after side markers. On next row, pm at first opening, CO 4 sts for armhole steek, pm, work to second opening, pm, CO 4 sts for armhole steek, pm. Dec 1 st at each side of armhole steeks EOR 10 (13, 16, 19) times. AT SAME TIME shape neck when piece measures 19 (21, 23, 24½)" from picot row.

Shape neck: BO 14 (16, 18, 15) sts on either side of front steek, and front steek sts. On next row, pm before neck edge, CO 4 neck steek sts, pm. Dec 1 st at each side of neck steek EOR 5 (5, 7, 11) times.

Cont working in patt until piece measures 20 (22, 24½, 27½)" from picot row.

Shape shoulders: On next row, BO neck steek sts, work to armhole steek, place sts for right front on holder, BO armhole steek, place sts for back on holder, BO second armhole steek, place sts for left front on holder.

Back shoulders: Place sts for back on needle and rejoin yarn. Working back and forth on only the back sts, BO 7 (8, 9, 11) sts at beg of next 2 rows. Work 14 (16, 18, 21) sts, join a second ball of yarn of each color, BO 36 (40, 48, 50) back neck sts, finish row. BO 7 (8, 9, 10) sts at beg of next row and dec 1 st each side of neck. BO 7 (8, 9, 10) sts at beg of next 3 rows.

Front shoulders: Place sts for right front on needle, rejoin yarn, and work shoulder shaping as for back. Rep shoulder shaping on left front sts.

Sleeves (Make 2)

With smaller needles and MC, CO 50 (58, 72, 78) sts. Work 6 rows in St st. Work picot row. Change to larger needles, purl 1 row, knit next row and pm, join into rnd being careful not to twist. Knit 4 more rnds. Beg chart B on st 23 (20, 1, 22) and rep rnds 30–53 of chart as necessary. Working incs into patt, inc 1 st on each side of marker every other rnd 0 (6, 12, 39) times, every 4 rnds 21 (19, 18, 6) times, then every 6 rnds 2 (0, 0, 0) times. Work even in patt until piece measures 14¼ (15½, 17, 18)".

Shape cap: BO 10 (14, 16, 20) sts, finish rnd and beg working back and forth. At beg of next row, BO 10 (14, 16, 20) sts, finish row. Dec 1 st at each side EOR 10 (13, 16, 19) times, then dec 1 st at each side every row 5 (3, 5, 11) times. BO 4 (4, 5, 7) sts at beg of next 4 rows. BO rem 30 (32, 38, 40) sts.

Finishing

For sample A, sew shoulder seams. Sew sleeves to body. Sew sleeve and side seams. For sample B, refer to "Steeks" (page 14) to cut steeks at armholes and on front. Sew shoulder seams. Sew sleeves to body and sew sleeve seams.

Neckband: With larger needles and MC, PU 14 (16, 18, 15) sts bound off from right front, 11 (11, 15, 25) sts from right neck, 44 (48, 56, 58) sts from back neck, 11 (11, 15, 25) sts from left neck, and 14 (16, 18, 15) sts bound off from left front—94 (102, 122, 138) sts. Work 5 rows in St st. Work picot row. Change to smaller needles and work 6 rows in St st. BO all sts.

Front bands: With larger needles and CC1, PU 96 (106, 116, 122) sts on front edge and work 5 rows in St st. Work picot row. Change to smaller needles and work 6 rows in St st. BO all sts. Rep on second front edge. Fold all edges to inside at picot rows and sew hems in place.

Weave in all ends and block as desired. Sew clasps to front bands.

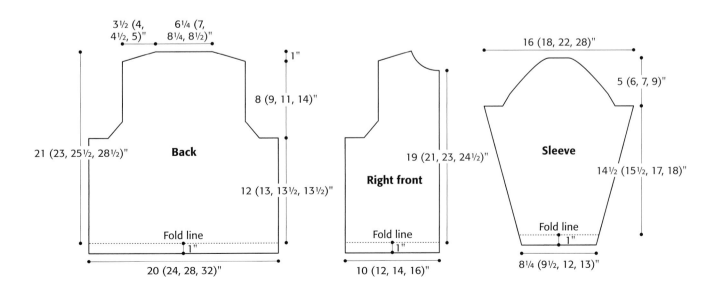

Chart A
(Worked back and forth)

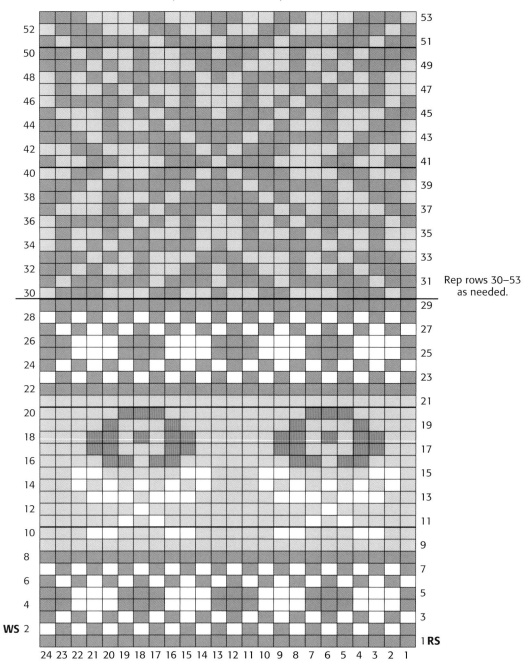

Rep rows 30–53
as needed.

Color key

MC

CC1

CC2

CC3

Chart B
(Worked in the round)

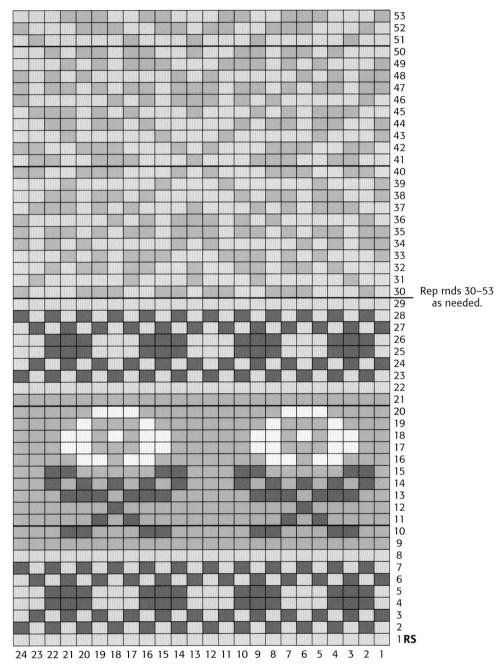

Rep rnds 30–53
as needed.

Color key

▢	MC
▢	CC1
▦	CC2
▢	CC3

Maureen Cardigan

Sample A

The simple openwork pattern provides visual interest, and it's also easy to knit.

Sample B

Yarn Notes: Both versions of this sweater are done in an unmercerized cotton. Mercerization is a process where cotton fibers are treated to improve their ability to absorb dye and its luster. Unmercerized cottons have a softer look and take on softer colors, as shown here. They also feel much softer against the skin.

Materials

Cotonade from Knit One, Crochet Too (100% cotton; 50 g; 83 yds) 🄸

Sample A

MC 8 (9, 11, 12, 15) balls • color 120

CC 2 (3, 3, 4, 5) balls • color 826

Sample B

MC 8 (9, 11, 12, 15) balls • color 337

CC 2 (3, 3, 4, 5) balls • color 531

Size 9 needles or size needed to obtain gauge

Size 8 circular needle (24")

Stitch markers

5 buttons, ⅞" diameter:

> **Sample A:** JHB International, Sandy Beach 87227

> **Sample B:** JHB International, Equator 90348

Gauge

16 sts and 20 rows = 4" in patt on larger needles

Flower Lace Pattern for Sizes Extra Small, Medium/Large, 2X/3X, and Sleeves

(multiple of 12 + 2)

Row 1 (RS): Knit.

Row 2 and all WS rows: Purl.

Row 3: K1, *K1, YO, sl 2 as if to knit, K1, p2sso, YO, K8, rep from *, end K1.

Row 5: K2tog, *YO, K3, YO, ssk, K5, K2tog, rep from * to last 12 sts, YO, K3, YO, ssk, K7.

Row 7: Rep row 3.

Row 9: Knit.

Row 11: Knit.

Row 13: K1, *K7, YO, sl 2 as if to knit, K1, p2sso, YO, K2, rep from *, end K1.

Row 15: K1, *K5, K2tog, YO, K3, YO, ssk, rep from *, end K1

Row 17: Rep row 13.

Row 19: Knit.

Row 20: Purl.

Rep rows 1–20 for patt.

Flower Lace Pattern for Sizes Small and 1X

(multiple of 12 + 8)

Row 1 (RS): Knit.

Row 2 and all WS rows: Purl.

Row 3: K4, *K1, YO, sl 2 as if to knit, K1, p2sso, YO, K8, rep from * to last 4 sts, K4.

Row 5: K2, K2tog, *YO, K3, YO, ssk, K5, K2tog, rep from * to last 4 sts, YO, K4.

Row 7: Rep row 3.

Row 9: Knit.

Row 11: Knit.

Row 13: K4, *K7, YO, sl 2 as if to knit, K1, p2sso, YO, K2, rep from * to last 4 sts, K4.

Row 15: K4, *K5, K2tog, YO, K3, YO, ssk, rep from * to last 4 sts, K4.

Row 17: Rep row 13.

Row 19: Knit.

Row 20: Purl.

Rep rows 1–20 for patt.

Back

With smaller needles and CC, CO 67 (71, 87, 93, 109) sts. Work in K1, P1 ribbing for 14 rows. On last row of ribbing, use M1 (page 12) to inc 7 (9, 11, 11, 13) sts evenly spaced—74 (80, 98, 104, 122) sts. Change to larger needles and MC, and beg flower lace patt for your size. Work in patt until piece measures 14 (16, 15½, 16, 16)" from beg, pm at each side to indicate underarms. Work in patt until piece measures 23 (25, 26, 27, 29)" from beg. BO all sts.

Fronts (Make 2, Reversing Shaping)

With smaller needles and CC, CO 33 (35, 43, 46, 54) sts. Work 14 rows in K1, P1 ribbing. On last row of ribbing, use M1 to inc 5 (5, 7, 6, 8) sts evenly spaced—38 (40, 50, 52, 62) sts. Change to larger needles and MC and beg flower lace patt for your size. Work in patt until piece measures 14 (16, 15½, 16, 16)" from beg, pm at side to indicate underarm.

Shape neck: Dec 1 st at neck edge EOR 4 (6, 5, 5, 2) times, then every 4 rows 8 (7, 9, 10, 14) times—26 (27, 36, 37, 46) sts. Work even in patt until piece measures 23 (25, 26, 27, 29)" from beg. BO all sts.

Sleeves (Make 2)

With smaller needles and CC, CO 29 (31, 33, 37, 45) sts. Work 14 rows in K1, P1 ribbing. On last row of ribbing, use K1f&b (page 12) to inc 3 (3, 5, 5, 5) sts evenly spaced—32 (34, 38, 42, 50) sts. Change to larger needles and MC. Purl 1 row, placing markers before and after the center 26 (26, 38, 38, 50) sts (for Medium/Large and 2X/3X, you will pm on either side of all sts on needle so far). Inc sts will be added outside these markers. On next row, beg working sts outside of markers in St st, and working sts between markers in flower lace patt. Work inc sts in St st until there are 13 sts at each end outside the markers. On next WS row, remove markers and place them after the first st and before the last st. Work sts between markers, including sts just added, in flower lace patt. Work new increased sts outside markers in St st, inc 1 st at each side EOR 7 (4, 9, 8, 12) times, every 4 rows 13 (15, 14, 15, 15) times—72 (72, 84, 88, 104) sts. Work even in patt until piece measures 16½ (16¾, 18, 18½, 20)" from beg. BO all sts.

Finishing

Sew shoulders.

Front and neck bands: With smaller needles and CC, beg at lower-right front edge, PU 57 (66, 65, 65, 65) sts to first neck dec, 36 (35, 40, 43, 52) sts along neck edge, 24 (26, 28, 30, 32) sts across back neck, 36 (35, 40, 43, 52) sts along left neck edge, and 57 (66, 65, 65, 65) sts along left front—210 (228, 238, 246, 268) sts. Work 4 rows in K1, P1 ribbing. On next RS row, work buttonholes as follows: work 2 sts, K2tog, YO, *work 12 (14, 14, 14, 14) sts, K2tog, YO, rep from * 4 times. Work 4 more rows in K1, P1 ribbing. BO all sts loosely in ribbing.

The directions for the buttonholes will result in a shallower V neck as shown in sample A on page 84. For a deeper V neck, space the buttonholes closer together. In sample B, there are a 9 stitches between each buttonhole.

Sew sleeves to armholes, sew side and sleeve seams. Sew buttons opposite buttonholes. Weave in all ends and block as desired.

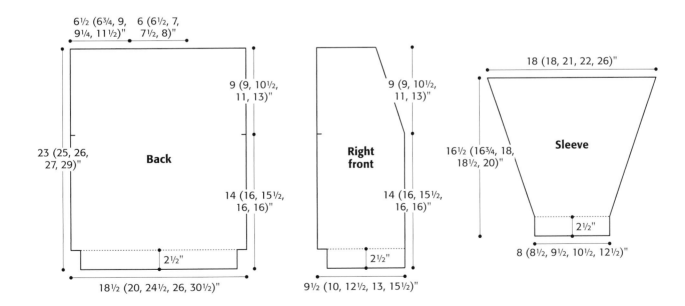

Back

6½ (6¾, 9, 9¼, 11½)"   6 (6½, 7, 7½, 8)"

9 (9, 10½, 11, 13)"

23 (25, 26, 27, 29)"

14 (16, 15½, 16, 16)"

2½"

18½ (20, 24½, 26, 30½)"

Right front

9 (9, 10½, 11, 13)"

14 (16, 15½, 16, 16)"

2½"

9½ (10, 12½, 13, 15½)"

Sleeve

18 (18, 21, 22, 26)"

16½ (16¾, 18, 18½, 20)"

2½"

8 (8½, 9½, 10½, 12½)"

Sandy Jacket

The garter stitch adds textural interest as well as flexibility to the sleeves and hood of this jacket.

Sample A

Sample B

Skill Level: Easy ◼◼◻◻

Size: Extra Small/Small (Medium, Large, 1X, 2X, 3X)

Finished Measurements:
Bust: 37 (41½, 47, 50½, 55, 58½)"
Length: 21 (22, 24, 25, 26, 27)"

Yarn Notes: Wool works well for this design because it offers warmth and lightness. Garter stitch in large quantities, such as the sleeves on this garment, can become very heavy when worked in some other types of yarns, and this could cause the sleeves to stretch out of shape. Some fibers worked in garter stitch might also be too bulky for comfortable elbow bending.

Materials

Cascade 220 from Cascade Yarns (100% wool; 100 g; 220 yds) ❨4❩

Sample A

MC 3 (3, 4, 4, 4, 4) balls • color 9444

CC 3 (3, 4, 4, 4, 4) balls • color 7827

Sample B

MC 3 (3, 4, 4, 4, 4) balls • color 8401

CC 3 (3, 4, 4, 4, 4) balls • color 8400

Size 9 needles or size needed to obtain gauge

Separating zipper in coordinating color in size to fit garment (or trim a longer zipper to fit)

Stitch markers

Gauge

17¾ sts and 22¾ rows = 4" in St st

19¼ sts and 32 rows = 4" in garter st

Back

With CC, CO 82 (93, 104, 113, 122, 131) sts. Work 4 rows in garter st. Change to MC and St st and work until piece measures 12 (12½, 13½, 14, 14, 14)" from beg, pm at each side to indicate underarms. Work until piece measures 21 (22, 24, 25, 26, 27)" from beg, BO all sts.

Fronts (Make 2, Reversing Shaping)

With CC, CO 41 (46, 52, 56, 61, 65) sts. Work 4 rows in garter st. Change to MC and St st, and work as for back until piece measures 18 (19, 21, 21½, 22½, 23½)" from beg.

Shape neck: At neck edge, BO 7 (7, 8, 8, 10, 10) sts, then dec 1 st at neck edge EOR 7 (7, 8, 8, 8, 8) times—27 (32, 36, 40, 43, 47) sts. Work even until piece measures 21 (22, 24, 25, 26, 27)" from beg. BO all sts.

Sleeves (Make 2)

With CC, CO 36 (38, 44, 48, 52, 58) sts. Working in garter st, inc 1 st at each side every 4 rows 9 (0, 14, 14, 23, 26) times, every 5 rows 0 (24, 0, 0, 0, 0) times, then every 6 rows 14 (0, 12, 12, 6, 4) times—82 (86, 96, 100, 110, 118) sts. Work even until piece measures 16 (16, 17, 17, 17, 17)" from beg. BO all sts.

Hood

Seam shoulders. With CC, PU 78 (82, 88, 94, 98, 98) sts around neck edge, pm in middle of back neck. Working in garter st, work even for 3 (3, 3, 3½, 3½, 3½)", then inc 1 st at each side of marker every 9 rows 6 (0, 0, 0, 0, 0) times, every 10 rows 2 (8, 0, 0, 0, 0) times, every 13 rows 0 (0, 4, 0, 0, 0) times, every 14 rows 0 (0, 2, 0, 0, 0) times, every 16 rows 0 (0, 0, 0, 5, 5) times, then every 40 rows 0 (0, 0, 2, 0, 0) times—94 (98, 100, 98, 108, 108) sts. When hood measures 12¼ (13, 13, 13½, 13½, 13½)" from PU row, place half of sts on second needle and work 3-needle BO (page 14).

Finishing

Front bands: With CC, PU 86 (90, 98, 102, 104, 110) sts along right front edge. Work 4 rows in garter st and BO all sts. Rep for left front edge.

Sew zipper to sweater fronts, in the valley between garter rows.

Sew sleeves to armholes, sew side and sleeve seams. Weave in all ends and block as desired.

A hood adds to the coziness of this casual design.

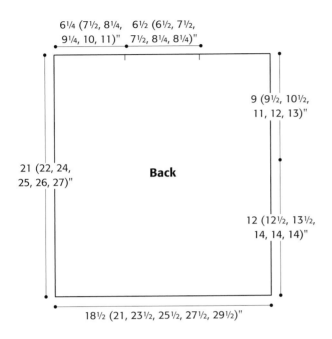

6¼ (7½, 8¼, 9¼, 10, 11)"   6½ (6½, 7½, 7½, 8¼, 8¼)"

9 (9½, 10½, 11, 12, 13)"

Back

21 (22, 24, 25, 26, 27)"

12 (12½, 13½, 14, 14, 14)"

18½ (21, 23½, 25½, 27½, 29½)"

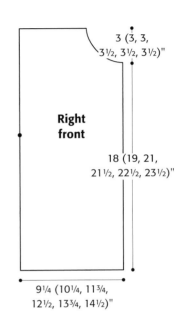

3 (3, 3, 3½, 3½, 3½)"

Right front

18 (19, 21, 21½, 22½, 23½)"

9¼ (10¼, 11¾, 12½, 13¾, 14½)"

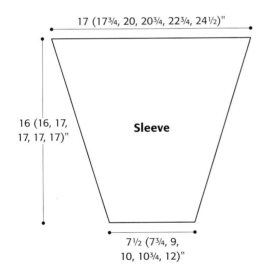

17 (17¾, 20, 20¾, 22¾, 24½)"

16 (16, 17, 17, 17, 17)"

Sleeve

7½ (7¾, 9, 10, 10¾, 12)"

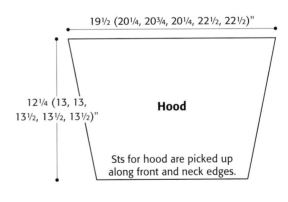

19½ (20¼, 20¾, 20¼, 22½, 22½)"

12¼ (13, 13, 13½, 13½, 13½)"

Hood

Sts for hood are picked up along front and neck edges.

Marilyn Poncho

Sample A

Sample B

The generous proportions of this design will fit most sizes, but the drape of the fabric makes it truly slimming.

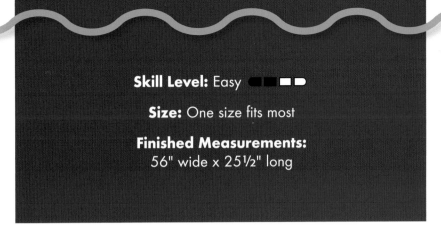

Skill Level: Easy ◖■■▯▷

Size: One size fits most

Finished Measurements:
56" wide x 25½" long

Yarn Notes: Besides being two different colors, the yarns used for these two versions are different textures, though they knit to the same gauge. The red yarn is a bouclé, which means it has slubs of yarn that make the strand thicker in some places and thinner in others. The gray yarn is smooth, adding to the more classic and subdued look of the piece.

Materials

Sample A

8 skeins of Color Waves from Lion Brand Yarn (83% acrylic, 17% polyester; 3 oz; 85 g; 125 yds; 113 m), color 313 Sunset Red ⑤

Size 10½ needles or size required to obtain gauge

Size 7 needles

Size 7 circular needle (16") or double-pointed needles

Sample B

6 balls of Wool-Ease Chunky from Lion Brand Yarn (80% acrylic, 20% wool; 5 oz; 140 g; 153 yds; 140 m), color 152 Charcoal ⑤

Size 13 needles or size required to obtain gauge

Size 9 needles

Size 9 circular needle (16") or double-pointed needles

Gauge

8½ sts and 13 rows = 4" in St st on larger needles for both samples A and B

Garter Edging Pattern

With smaller needles, knit 1 row.

With larger needles, knit 1 row.

Rep these 2 rows once more.

Slanted Ribbing Pattern

Worked in the round

Rnd 1: *YO, K2tog, rep from * around.

Rep this rnd.

Back

With larger needles, CO 119 sts. Work garter edging. Cont using larger needles and work in St st until piece measures 25½" from beg. BO all sts.

Front

Work as for back until piece measures 22" from beg. Work 55 sts, join second ball of yarn and BO 9 sts, finish row. BO 2 sts at each neck edge EOR twice. Work each side until same length as back. Then BO 51 sts across each shoulder.

Finishing

Sew shoulder seams. Using circular needle or dpn, PU 44 sts around neck edge. Work in slanted rib for 4". BO very loosely. With larger needles, PU 112 sts along right edge of poncho, work garter edging and BO all sts. Rep on opposite side. At each side, join front and back pieces starting 10" down from shoulder seam and sew a seam for 5", leaving the bottom edges open. Weave in all ends and block as desired.

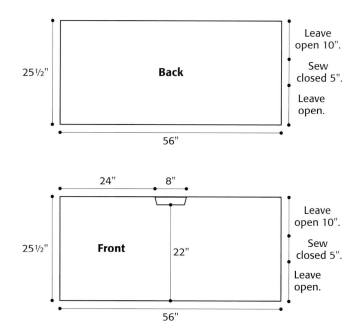

A Note about Ponchos

This poncho may seem like two shapeless blankets while you're making it, but the fabric drapes or forms to your body. When you put it on, the fabric will fold along your shape and actually have a slimming effect!

Ponchos are versatile pieces in any wardrobe. They can be dressed up for an evening of fun, or thrown over a turtleneck for a cozy wrap on a rainy Sunday afternoon. Embellishments such as a glittery pin or a silk flower can add a bit of spark to the solid-colored poncho. Adding fringe, like on the Virginia Scarf on page 102, is another way to give a poncho a fresh look. The Virginia Scarf fringe includes silver-lined beads, but you could choose different beads or no beads at all. And if you like the effect of a fuzzy edge, use novelty yarn for the garter edging instead of the yarn specified in the project instructions.

This is a great project for a beginner—lots and lots of stockinette, some easy garter stitch, and the slightest of shaping. Since it's one-size-fits-most, there's no worry about getting a perfect gauge or measurements. It's a first-time project the knitter will be proud to wear!

A simple stitch pattern produces an intricate-looking neck detail.

Eleanor Cape

Sample A

Sample B

Everyone needs a velvety cape
for dramatic or elegant occasions
(or for everyday wear).

Yarn Notes: This yarn is perfect to wear if you want to be touched! Its softness and smoothness can make it a bit slippery, so you may want to use bamboo or wood needles with some grip. You may also find it helpful to keep the working yarn in a plastic bag with a closure to keep it from slipping away.

Materials

Sinsation from Plymouth Yarn Company (80% rayon, 20% wool; 50 g; 38 yds) (4)

Sample A

MC 15 skeins • color 3351

CC 4 skeins • color 3301

Sample B

MC 10 skeins • color 3375

CC 3 skeins • color 3300

Size 10½ circular needle (36" long) or size required to obtain gauge

2 frog closures for sample A, 1 closure for sample B

Stitch markers

Sewing needle and thread

Gauge

10 sts and 12 rows = 4" in St st

Cape

Cape is worked in one piece from the neck down.

With MC, CO 26 sts. K1, pm, K1, pm, K4, pm, K1, pm, K12, pm, K1, pm, K4, pm, K1, pm, K1. Purl 1 row.

Shape neck

Row 1: *Knit to marker, sl marker, M1, K1, sl marker, M1, rep from * 3 more times, knit to end—34 sts.

Row 2: Purl.

Row 3: Rep row 1—42 sts.

Row 4: Purl.

Shape shoulder

Row 1: K1, M1, *knit to marker, M1, slip marker, K1 (seam st), sl marker, M1, rep from * 3 more times, knit to last st, M1, K1—52 sts.

Row 2: Purl.

Row 3: Rep row 1—62 sts.

Row 4: Purl.

Shape body: CO 3 sts, work row 1 of shoulder shaping WITHOUT inc after first and before last st. CO 3 sts. Purl 1 row. St count should be as follows: 11 sts, marker, seam st, marker, 14 sts, marker, seam st, marker, 22 sts, marker, seam st, marker, 14 sts, marker, seam st, marker, 11 sts—76 sts.

Inc row: M1 on either side of each seam st. Work inc row EOR 8 times, then every 4 rows until cape is 11½ (23½)" from beg (or desired length less 1½"). Change to CC and work 1½" in garter st. BO all sts.

Finishing

Hoodless cape: With RS of cape facing you and CC, PU 16 sts from right front neck, 12 sts from back neck, and 16 sts from left front neck—44 sts. Work 1½" in garter st. BO all sts loosely. With CC, PU 64 sts along right front edge. (This number will be different if you altered the length. Try to PU about 3 sts for every 4 rows.) Work 1½" in garter st. BO all sts. Rep on second side. Sew on frogs with sewing needle and thread.

Hooded cape: With RS of cape facing you and MC, PU 16 sts from right front neck, 6 sts from right half of back neck, pm, PU 6 sts from left side of back neck, and 16 sts from left front neck—44 sts. Purl 1 row. Working back and forth, work even for 3", then inc 1 st at each side of marker every 4 rows 5 times, then every 5 rows 4 times—62 sts. Work even until piece measures 13", place half of sts on a separate needle and work 3-needle BO (page 14). With CC, PU 34 sts along right front edge, 65 sts along front edge of hood, and 34 sts along left front edge—133 sts. (This number will be different if you altered the length. Try to PU about 3 sts for every 4 rows.) Work 1½" in garter st. BO all sts. Sew on frog(s) with needle and thread.

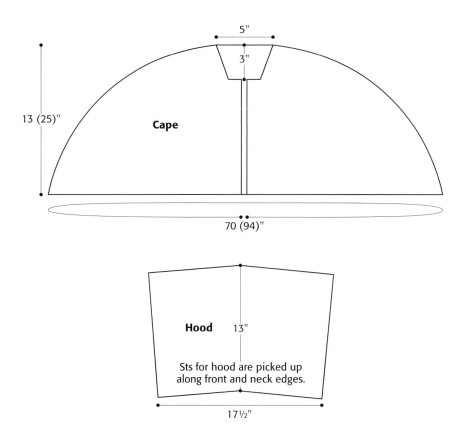

5"

3"

13 (25)"

Cape

70 (94)"

Hood 13"

Sts for hood are picked up along front and neck edges.

17½"

The hood can be added to or omitted from either version, and you can make the cape any length you wish (try it on while you're making it).

Virginia Scarf

Sample A

Is it a scarf? Is it a shawl?
The choice is yours.

Sample B

Yarn Notes: The contrasting styles of these two yarns give very different effects. The green version is in a shiny cotton/modal blend, and can be worn to add a punch of spring color to a winter ensemble or as a shawl with a summer dress. The gray version adds subtle texture to a winter coat or works as a winter evening shawl.

Materials

Sample A

3 skeins of Shine from Knit Picks (60% cotton, 40% modal; 50 g; 110 yds), color 6561 Green Apple **2**

Sample B

3 balls of Wool Cotton from Rowan Yarns (50% wool, 50% cotton; 50 g; 123 yds), color 903 Misty **2**

Size 9 needles or size required to obtain gauge

Optional: about 500 silver-lined beads, size 4 mm, for fringe; medium crochet hook for fringe

Gauge

12¾ sts and 20 rows = 4" in patt st

Virginia Lace Pattern

(multiple of 6 + 1)

Row 1 and all odd-numbered rows (WS): Purl.

Row 2: K1, *K1, YO, ssk, YO, ssk, K1, rep from *.

Row 4: K1, *K2, YO, ssk, YO, ssk, rep from *.

Row 6: *Ssk, K2, YO, ssk, YO, rep from *, end K1.

Row 8: K2, *K2, YO, ssk, YO, ssk, rep from * to last 5 sts, K2, YO, ssk, K1.

Row 10: K1, *YO, ssk, K2, YO, ssk, rep from *.

Row 12: K2, *YO, ssk, K2, YO, ssk, rep from * to last 5 sts, YO, ssk, K3.

Row 14: K3, *YO, ssk, K2, YO, ssk, rep from * to last 4 sts, YO, ssk, K2.

Rep rows 1–14 for patt.

To make a narrower scarf, use smaller needles or cast on fewer stitches. To make a wider shawl, use larger needles or cast on more stitches. If you vary the number of cast-on stitches, you must use a number equal to a multiple of 6 plus 1; for example, one less repeat would be 43 stitches, and one more repeat would be 55 stitches.

Scarf (or Shawl)

CO 49 sts, work in Virginia lace patt until piece measures 50" or desired length. BO all sts loosely.

Finishing

Block finished piece. I used a steam iron and actually ironed the pieces lightly from the back, but you can wash the piece and stretch it out with pins to dry if you prefer.

Optional fringe: Cut 196 pieces of yarn each 12" long. Holding 2 pieces tog, fold them in half, and use a crochet hook to pull the fold through 1 st on the CO edge, then pull the ends through the fold. Rep in each st along CO and BO edges. Slide 1 or 2 beads on each end of fringe and tie in a knot. I have found that beads slip over knots, no matter how big the knot, unless I knot the yarn around the bead itself, but your experience may differ.

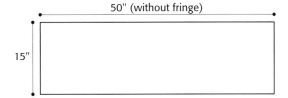

50" (without fringe)

15"

Leave your fringe unbeaded for a soft shower of yarn, or try one of the following options if you'd like an eye-catching finish.

- Add silver-lined teardrop beads as shown for subtle punch.

- Attach large, chunky beads for a stronger statement.

- Vary bead shapes for a funky look.

- Consider coordinating or contrasting bead colors with the yarn, depending on the look you want.

- Knot beads along the length of the fringe or tie them only at the ends.

Constance Scarf

Sample A

Sample B

Make two scarves for the work of one—brighten a gray day with the pink side. or keep things neutral with the gray. Knit a pink strip and join it to a grey one. then display whichever side suits your mood when you wear the finished scarf.

Yarn Notes: The super-bulky yarn makes this scarf quick to knit, and the double thickness makes it very warm. It is surprisingly light, however, because the wool is loosely spun. The gray side uses two different shades of gray for more textural definition, while the pink yarn already includes subtle variations in tone. If you prefer, knit one strip for a single-colored scarf.

Materials

Rowan Big Wool from Rowan Yarns (100% merino wool; 100 g; 80 m) 🄖

MC 2 balls • color 31 Smooch

CC1 1 ball • color 07 Smoky

CC2 1 ball • color 19 Smudge

Two size 17 circular needles (24" or longer) or size required to obtain gauge

Size P (15 mm) crochet hook

Gauge

6½ sts and 12 rows = 4" in patt st

Solid-Color Pattern

(multiple of 2 + 2)

Row 1: *K1, P1, rep from * to last st, K1.

Row 2: Knit.

Rep rows 1 and 2 for patt.

Two-Color Pattern

(multiple of 2 + 1)

Row 1: With CC1, *K1, P1, rep from * to last st, K1, slide sts to other end of needle.

Row 2: With CC2, knit all sts, turn work.

Row 3: With CC1, *P1, K1, rep from * to last st, P1, slide sts to other end of needle.

Row 4: With CC2, purl all sts, turn work.

Rep rows 1–4 for patt.

Scarf

Using provisional CO (page 12) and MC, CO 99 sts. Work solid-color patt for 18 rows. On second needle, using provisional CO and CC1, CO 99 sts. Work two-color patt for 16 rows once, then rep first 2 rows once more.

Finishing

Place 2 needles holding sts tog. Use MC and 3-needle BO (page 14) to join pieces. Remove provisional CO from opposite side of each piece, place these sts on 2 separate needles and BO with MC as other side. Leave shorter ends open so scarf can be turned inside out for a different look.

61"

6"

Abbreviations Glossary

approx	approximately
beg	begin(ning)
BO	bind off
C4B	cable 4 back
C4F	cable 4 front
C6B	cable 6 back
C6F	cable 6 front
CC	contrasting color
cn	cable needle
CO	cast on
cont	continue(ing)
dec(s)	decrease(s)(ing)
dpn	double-pointed needles
EOR	every other row
g	grams
garter st	garter stitch (knit every row)
inc(s)	increase(s)(ing)
K	knit
K1f&b	knit into front and back of same stitch (1 stitch increase; page 12)
K1tbl	knit 1 stitch through the back loop
K2tog	knit 2 stitches together (1 stitch decrease)
LC	left cross
LT	left twist
M1	make 1 stitch (1 stitch increase; page 12)
MC	main color
P	purl
P1tbl	purl 1 stitch through the back loop
P2tog	purl 2 stitches together (1 stitch decrease)
patt	pattern

pm	place marker
p2sso	pass 2 slipped stitches over
psso	pass slipped stitch over
PU	pick up and knit with RS facing you unless instructed otherwise
RC	right cross
RT	right twist
rem	remain(s)(ing)
rep	repeat(s)
rev St st	reverse Stockinette stitch (purl on right side, knit on wrong side)
rnd(s)	round(s)
RS	right side
sl	slip
ssk	slip, slip, knit (slip next stitch as if to knit, slip next stitch as if to knit, knit these 2 stitches together through the back loops; 1 stitch decrease)
ssp	slip, slip, purl (slip next stitch as if to knit, slip next stitch as if to knit, purl these 2 stitches together through the back loops; 1 stitch decrease)
st(s)	stitch(es)
St st	Stockinette stitch (knit on right side, purl on wrong side)
T3B	twist 3 back
T3F	twist 3 front
tbl	through back loop
WS	wrong side
wyib	with yarn in back
yds	yards
YO	yarnover

Useful Information

The Craft Yarn Council of America has developed a set of standards and guidelines for crochet and knitting. As a part of their efforts to standardize directions, they have developed guidelines for skill levels and yarn weights. These guidelines and their icons are used throughout this book.

Skill Levels

■□□□ **Beginner:** projects for first-time knitters using basic knit and purl stitches. Minimal shaping.

■■□□ **Easy:** projects using basic stitches, repetitive stitch patterns, and simple color changes. Simple shaping and finishing.

■■■□ **Intermediate:** projects with a variety of stitches, such as basic cables and lace, simple intarsia, double-pointed needles, and knitting in the round techniques. Midlevel shaping and finishing.

■■■■ **Experienced:** projects using advanced techniques and stitches, such as short rows fair isle, more intricate intarsia, cables, lace patterns, and numerous color changes.

Needle Sizes

Needle sizes in this book are listed in U.S. needle sizes. Consult the chart to find the equivalent metric size.

U.S. Size	Metric Size (mm)
1	2.25
2	2.75
3	3.25
4	3.5
5	3.75
6	4
7	4.5
8	5
9	5.5
10	6
10½	6.5
11	8
13	9
15	10
17	12.75

Yarn Weights

Yarn-Weight Symbol and Category Names	1 Super fine	2 Fine	3 Light	4 Medium	5 Bulky	6 Super bulky
Type of Yarns in Category	Sock, Fingering, Baby	Sport, Baby	DK, Light Worsted	Worsted, Afghan, Aran	Chunky, Craft, Rug	Bulky, Roving
Knit Gauge Ranges in Stockinette Stitch to 4"	27 to 32 sts	23 to 26 sts	21 to 24 sts	16 to 20 sts	12 to 15 sts	6 to 11 sts
Recommended Needle in U.S. Size Range	1 to 3	3 to 5	5 to 7	7 to 9	9 to 11	11 and larger

Measurements

Use these handy formulas for easy conversions.

Yards x .91 = meters

Meters x 1.09 = yards

Grams x .035 = ounces

Ounces x 28.35 = grams

Bibliography

Carroll, Amy, ed. *The Pattern Library: Knitting.* New York: Ballantine Books, 1981. *Stitch treasury, including the cross and stripe pattern adapted for Ruth Jacket.*

Klopper, Gisela. *Beautiful Knitting Patterns* New York: Sterling Books, 2001. *Stitch treasury, including designs adapted for Rose Camisole, Marie Turtleneck, and Cecile Vest.*

Walker, Barbara G. *A Treasury of Knitting Patterns.* Pittsville, WI: Schoolhouse Press, 1998. *A compendium of knitting patterns, including the basis for the star rib mesh used in Sue Tunic and the royal quilting in Edna Vest.*

Wiseman, Nancie M. *The Knitter's Book of Finishing Techniques.* Woodinville, WA: Martingale & Company, 2002. *More than just finishing techniques, this book is a comprehensive resource for knitting techniques of all kinds.*

Resources

Contact the following companies to find shops that carry the yarns and buttons featured in this book.

Alchemy Yarns of Transformation

www.alchemyyarns.com

Bamboo, Lone Star, Synchronicity

Blue Sky Alpacas

www.blueskyalpacas.com

Blue Sky Cotton, Organic Cotton

Cascade Yarns

www.cascadeyarns.com

Cascade 220, Cotton Rich, Di.Vé Teseo

Cherry Tree Hill Yarns

www.cherryyarn.com

Silk and Merino Worsted

Dale of Norway

www.daleofnorway.com

Falk, Free Style Dalegarn, Heilo

Dawn Brocco

www.dawnbrocco.com

Clasps for Alice jackets

JHB International

www.buttons.com

Buttons for Maureen and Jayne cardigans

Knit One, Crochet Too

www.knitonecrochettoo.com

Cotonade

Knit Picks

www.knitpicks.com

Andean Silk, Shimmer, Shine

Lion Brand Yarn

www.lionbrandyarn.com

Color Waves, Microspun, Wool-Ease, Wool-Ease Chunky

Plymouth Yarn Company

www.plymouthyarn.com

Galway, Galway Colornep, Royal Cashmere, Sinsation

Rowan Yarns

www.knitrowan.com

Rowan Big Wool, Kid Classic, Wool Cotton, Yorkshire Tweed Aran

Knitting and Crochet Titles

Martingale® & COMPANY

CROCHET

Classic Crocheted Vests
Crochet from the Heart NEW!
Crochet for Babies and Toddlers
Crochet for Tots
Crocheted Aran Sweaters
Crocheted Lace
Crocheted Socks!
Crocheted Sweaters
First Crochet NEW!
Fun and Funky Crochet NEW!
The Little Box of Crocheted Hats and Scarves
More Crocheted Aran Sweaters NEW!
Today's Crochet

KNITTING

200 Knitted Blocks
365 Knitting Stitches a Year: Perpetual Calendar
Basically Brilliant Knits
Beyond Wool
Big Knitting NEW!
Classic Knitted Vests
Comforts of Home
Dazzling Knits
Fair Isle Sweaters Simplified
First Knits
Garden Stroll, A
Handknit Style
Knit It Now!
Knits for Children and Their Teddies
Knits from the Heart
Knitted Shawls, Stoles, and Scarves

Knitted Throws and More for the Simply Beautiful Home
The Knitter's Book of Finishing Techniques
A Knitter's Template
Knitting with Hand-Dyed Yarns
Knitting with Novelty Yarns
Lavish Lace
The Little Box of Knitted Ponchos and Wraps NEW!
The Little Box of Knitted Throws NEW!
The Little Box of Scarves
The Little Box of Scarves II
The Little Box of Sweaters
More Paintbox Knits
Perfectly Brilliant Knits NEW!
The Pleasures of Knitting
Pursenalities
Rainbow Knits for Kids
Sarah Dallas Knitting
Saturday Sweaters NEW!
Sensational Knitted Socks NEW!
Simply Beautiful Sweaters
Simply Beautiful Sweaters for Men
Style at Large
A Treasury of Rowan Knits
The Ultimate Knitted Tee
The Ultimate Knitter's Guide

Our books are available at bookstores and your favorite craft, fabric, and yarn retailers. If you don't see the title you're looking for, visit us at
www.martingale-pub.com or contact us at:

1-800-426-3126

International: 1-425-483-3313
Fax: 1-425-486-7596
Email: info@martingale-pub.com